Teaching
the Brain to
READ

JUDY WILLIS, M.D.

Teaching the Brain to

READ

Strategies for Improving Fluency,
Vocabulary, and Comprehension

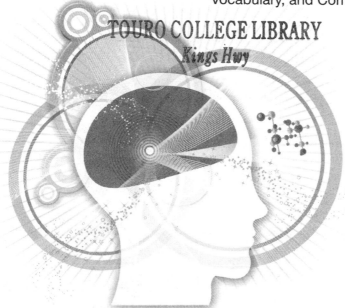

Association for Supervision and Curriculum Development
Alexandria, Virginia USA

KH

Association for Supervision and Curriculum Development
1703 N. Beauregard St. • Alexandria, VA 22311-1714 USA
Phone: 800-933-2723 or 703-578-9600 • Fax: 703-575-5400
Web site: www.ascd.org • E-mail: member@ascd.org
Author guidelines: www.ascd.org/write

Gene R. Carter, *Executive Director;* Nancy Modrak, *Director of Publishing;* Julie Houtz, *Director of Book Editing & Production;* Deborah Siegel, *Project Manager;* Greer Beeken, *Senior Graphic Designer;* Mike Kalyan, *Production Manager;* Marlene Hochberg, *Typesetter*

All Web links in this book are correct as of the publication date below but may have become inactive or otherwise modified since that time. If you notice a deactivated or changed link, please e-mail books@ascd.org with the words "Link Update" in the subject line. In your message, please specify the Web link, the book title, and the page number on which the link appears.

PAPERBACK ISBN: 978-1-4166-0688-8 ASCD product #107073   s8/08
Also available as an e-book through ebrary, netLibrary, and many online booksellers (see Books in Print for the ISBNs).

Quantity discounts for the paperback edition only: 10–49 copies, 10%; 50+ copies, 15%; for 1,000 or more copies, call 800-933-2723, ext. 5634, or 703-575-5634. For desk copies: member@ascd.org.

Library of Congress Cataloging-in-Publication Data

Willis, Judy.
  Teaching the brain to read : strategies for improving fluency, vocabulary, and comprehension / Judy Willis.
      p. cm.
  Includes bibliographical references and index.
  ISBN 978-1-4166-0688-8 (pbk. : alk. paper) 1. Reading. 2. Reading—Physiological aspects. 3. Brain. I. Title.

  LB1573. W544 2008
  428.4—dc22

                            2008015658

18 17 16 15 14 13 12 11 10 09 08   1 2 3 4 5 6 7 8 9 10 11 12

2/9/10

~

To my mom, Norma Allerhand, whose love of reading
is only exceeded by the love she has for her family.

~

Teaching the Brain to Read

Preface viii

Acknowledgments xiv

Introduction 1

1. From Syllable to Synapse:
   Prereading Through Decoding 11

2. Patterning Strategies 22

3. Fluency Building from the Brain to the Book 47

4. Eliminating Barriers on the Road to Fluency........... 68

5. Vocabulary Building and Keeping 80

6. Successful Reading Comprehension 126

Conclusion 157

Glossary 159

References 163

Index 170

About the Author 175

Preface

In 1990, George Bush signed a proclamation declaring that the upcoming decade would be "The Decade of the Brain." The proclamation stated that the coming years would "Enhance public awareness of the benefits to be derived from brain research appropriate programs, ceremonies, and activities." In fact, the amount of learning-related brain research completed in that decade through neuroimaging exceeded all prior brain imaging studies devoted to educational research. Yet with all the data from that decade and the continued research of the past seven years, the scientific and educational communities have not reached agreement on the best way to teach reading.

What the research has provided is a wealth of information about how the brain responds to the written word, which areas of the brain are most active during the complex processes of reading, and some of the strategies that seem to increase brain activity and efficiency. The most difficult part is to correlate brain scan activity with objective qualitative improvement in reading skill. The educational literature is saturated with reading controversies that sometimes mix fact with opinion or interpret data with biased, propitiatory interpretations. The goal to strive for is objective data from functional brain imaging that objectively correlates with cognitive response to specific reading strategies.

The more information provided from the research about how the brain learns to read better, more efficiently, and with more intrinsic motivation, the greater the expectations that will be placed upon teachers to keep up with this research information and the strategies that are derived from it. Parents read about reading breakthroughs in parenting books and magazines and don't hesitate to express their expectations to their children's teachers and school administrators. Rightfully so. In the 15 years I practiced adult and child neurology before returning to university for my teaching certification and Master of Education degree, I expected parents to be active partners in my neurological evaluations and treatments of their children. As I've written before, no parent of a child with epilepsy ever came to my neurology office and said, "Just do what you think is best without explaining my child's condition or your approach to me. Whatever happens to my child is all in your hands because you are the expert neurologist and I'm *just* the parent."

If parents were so removed from their child's medical care I would have been concerned about that child's well being. Similarly, as teachers we can and should expect parents to be advocates for their children, especially with the most critical of all academic skills—reading. With this book I will offer a background in the brain research related to how the "average" brain is activated sequentially as data passes along neuronal networks to the multiple processing centers that are engaged in sequence from the time print is seen on a page to various culminating actions such as verbal or written response to what was read (reading comprehension and critical analysis). Just as physicians are not specialists in all fields, general educators cannot become experts in all areas of reading difficulties and differences. There will always be the need for reading specialists. Yet, just as involved parents become allied with the physician to partner in their children's medical care, teachers with an understanding of the research about reading problems and remedial strategies will be in the best position to partner with the reading specialists, families, and students to make the process of learning to read as successful as possible. It will then fall primarily upon classroom teachers to use the art of teaching to instill in their students the love of reading.

As educators, we are in the privileged position to recognize that the learning process never ends. Just as science is always questioning itself, professional educators continue to examine, test, deconstruct, and reconstruct strategies to become better at the important job we are entrusted with. In this time of brain research focused on learning, and especially learning to read, we are in the exciting position of having neuroimaging that shows us what takes place in which parts of the brain when the intake of sensory information is successfully encoded and passes from sensory response regions through the emotional limbic system filters and on through to short term, working, relational, and ultimately long-term memory storage. We can see on scans and special quantitative electroencephalogram recordings what strategies culminate in increased metabolic activity in the visual response centers, relational processing regions, long-term storage areas, and frontal lobe regions known to become active during executive functioning (highest level processing of information gained from reading such that it is used to form judgments, prioritize, analyze, and conceptualize).

When my daughter Malana was a student in education graduate school she acknowledged the difficulties that lay ahead but also wrote to me about the opportunities, "Teaching is not meant to be a practice in perfection. Rather it is an opportunity to continuously grow, learn, ask questions, be confused, and overcome challenges. Teaching is an especially collaborative effort. It is the classroom teacher's responsibility to work with the student, the family and a variety of professionals as part of a group to make learning to read a positive experience for all."

That is what I hope to encourage with this book—to provide the opportunity for educators to read about the latest research about how the brain reads and build enough background knowledge to form opinions about which studies seem valid and which appear biased. As you increase your understanding about the current state of brain-based reading research, you will be able to select carefully from future research claims and apply the results to develop additional classroom instruction strategies based on the new research to further promote reading success in all of your students.

The first chapters will focus on what has been concluded or deduced about the brain's processing of the written or spoken word including what differences in children's brain scans correlate with their reading successes or difficulties in the distinct aspects of the complex act of reading. This will lead into chapters about the influence of stress on the development of reading and fluency skills and neuroimaging research and strategies to improve reading comprehension and vocabulary.

Brain research has shown us the positive and negative impact of students' emotional states on the affective filter in their amygdalas. This original work related to Krashen's research on the affective filter revealed the stressors that impaired and delayed English language learning in non-English speaking students in American schools. Through neuroimaging, there is now evidence confirming the importance of preventing metabolic overload of the brain's affective filter in the emotional-limbic system. Strategies will be provided to help students maintain the ideal state of emotional homeostasis needed for sounds and words to enter the brain's reading comprehension pathways without being blocked by this affective filter. This information will be built upon with the brain compatible strategies that provide students with the motivation to persevere with the challenges of improving their reading proficiency.

Brain research compatible whole class and individualized reading activities will be detailed including specific examples of multi-disciplinary units of reading across the curriculum, techniques for building reading comprehension and memory, and strategies for bringing newly acquired knowledge from reading into the highest cognitive function regions of the brain's frontal lobe where this information is used to make the connections, comparisons, and analyses that represent judgment and wisdom. Also offered will be the strategies that encourage students to choose to read in our time of the powerful siren's call of multimedia games, videos, and Internet surfing.

The emphasis of this book will be the brain research and associated strategies for reading instruction beyond decoding. The first chapter will provide a review of what has come before and preview of the possible strategies to come by describing the strongest validated research in the neuroscience regarding the earliest parts of the reading process. This chapter will therefore briefly review things like alphabetic knowledge, phoneme-to-grapheme correspondences, and use of phonetic cues to decode words as a lead-in to the main emphasis of the book—how the brain learns to read beyond decoding.

Beyond Decoding

In subjects such as brain patterning of information, development of reading fluency, vocabulary building, reading comprehension, and long-term memory storage of information learned from reading, the research is more specific and gaining more support from multicenter confirmation of data. Similarly the strategies suggested by this postdecoding research are more defined. It is therefore the strategies that coincide with the brain's activities that follow decoding that will be the emphasis of this book.

These are the parts of the reading process when the brain links the abstract orthographic representations it decodes with its system of phonological codes. This is when patterning begins to take the decoded words and process them into comprehensible categories and when words and phrases are associated with meanings in the process of developing fluent reading. Simultaneously, word vocabulary is increasing and strategies are available to facilitate vocabulary-building skills. Ultimately the patterning of phonological coding, enriched by greater vocabulary, combines with the increased fluency to reach the later reading stages of comprehension of increasingly complex text.

Included in each chapter will be the background brain termi-nology for teachers less specialized in the science of reading. This will be a review of the research that has stood the test of time and has been confirmed by multicenter testing. That background will be followed by my description of the cutting edge research from smaller studies too new to have been reproduced at other centers. This is the work carried out by the experienced and respected research groups whose work I have followed for over a decade. This is the brain-learning research that was conducted with such atten-tion to controlling variables and confirming evidence and with no link to vested interest groups, that in my opinion it will be the research that becomes doctrine. Some of this more complex infor-mation will be set aside in sidebars designated *Gray Matter*.

Accompanying the research I review will be the implications for teaching and learning—the specific neuro *logical* strategies that support what the brain reading research interpretations suggest. Some of this information has already been supported by follow-up neuroimaging and cognitive testing.

Throughout the book there will be detailed, explicitly described strategies presented as step-by-step activities adaptable for differ-ent grade levels, taken from my classroom and ready for educators to apply in their classrooms today. It is my hope that these brain research compatible techniques can help other educators as they have helped me to increase students' motivation to read and enjoy the wealth of pleasure and knowledge available to people who develop a lifelong love affair with reading.

Acknowledgments

To Paul, my husband, for encouraging my career change, the writing of my books, and my travels to distant cities where I speak. Nothing in my life is complete until I have shared it with you. To Malana and Alani Willis, my daughters who fill me with love and laughter and remind me what happens when children have wonderful teachers. To all my colleagues at Santa Barbara Middle School, for their enduring passion for teaching from their hearts and minds. To all of my students at Santa Barbara Middle School, especially those who visit my classroom when they are no longer in my class, and their parents who support education within and beyond the classroom door.

To Scott Willis, Deborah Siegel, and David Snyder at ASCD, without whom my ideas could not reach the page.

To my teachers and yours, whose patient instruction enables us to read these words.

Introduction

On a hot day, after a climb up a few hundred steps in a historic lighthouse on the Oregon coast, I was weary but ready for the next adventure. I was motivated because I knew it was worth climbing those stairs for the view from the top. In the parking lot I heard a boy of about 5 complain to his parents in the overtired and frustrated whine any parent or teacher recognizes. He didn't want to go to any more lighthouses. They were "stupid and boring," so why should he have to go? As the child became more angry and resistant, his parents suggested that he could sit in the car and calm down and then they could continue the discussion. This boy knew what that meant. He knew there would be no discussion and he would have no say in the outcome, so he just snapped and said, "Sitting isn't leaving!"

The emotions he was feeling are much like those of children who struggle with learning to read and later learning to understand complex text. The frustration, the anxiety about making mistakes, and the impatience build and build as teachers and parents try to coerce the child to climb the lighthouse steps that are the "must-know spelling words."

Reading comes easily to some children, but most struggle with some part of the complex process that begins with phonemes and continues to comprehension of complex text. When students are asked to face stressful reading challenges, they don't feel good about the reading equivalent of a hot day and a daunting staircase.

They will be resistant when the task they are asked to do is either not at their skill level or so unmotivating that they can't or won't persevere. They also don't necessarily value the reward, be it the view from the lighthouse or the reading of a book. They may not think that there is any purpose in struggling to read when they can enjoy stories and even acquire information from videos, movies, television, and being read to. Asking a child to just suck up reading frustration won't work.

Reading is not a natural part of human development. Unlike spoken language, reading does not follow from observation and imitation of other people (Jacobs, Schall, & Scheibel, 1993). Specific regions of the brain are devoted to processing oral communication, but there are no specific regions of the brain dedicated to reading. The complexity of reading requires multiple areas of the brain to operate together through networks of neurons. This means there are many potential brain dysfunctions that can interfere with reading.

Considering all the cognitive tasks required to go from connecting symbols to sounds, sounds to words, words to meaning, meaning to memory, and memory to thoughtful information processing, it is not surprising that an estimated 20 percent to 35 percent of American elementary through high school students experience significant reading difficulties (Schneider & Chein, 2003).

I am filled with awe and respect for every teacher who has helped a student climb the lighthouse stairs by using successful strategies and motivators. Without these teachers, children would never discover that the view from the top is so wonderful.

The Development of Brain-Based Research

The two most important advances in brain-based research are positron emission tomography (PET) and functional magnetic resonance imaging (fMRI). The PET scan relies on one of the brain's properties; it is extremely hungry for glucose and oxygen. PET scans measure the metabolism of glucose in the brain in response to certain activities. In this technique, positron–emitting isotopes, which function as radioactive tracers, are injected into the arteries in combination with glucose. The rate at which specific regions of the brain use the glucose is recorded while the subject is engaged in various sorts of cognitive activities. These recordings are used to produce maps of areas of high and low brain activity with particular cognitive functions.

The technology behind fMRI is similar to that of MRI. However, fMRI takes advantage of a special property of hemoglobin, a blood protein that brings oxygen to body tissues. Hemoglobin that is carrying oxygen has different properties from hemoglobin that is not carrying oxygen. By detecting oxygen-containing hemoglobin, scientists use fMRI to assess changes in blood flow to areas of the brain. Active regions of the brain receive more blood and more oxygen.

Specifically, fMRI has been prominent in revealing the neural mechanisms for reading in children. The PET scans have limitations because of radioactivity of the isotope used in the tracer material injected. The fMRI is completely painless, does not involve radiation, and is also faster. It does have the problem of being very loud, but researchers have found that if they precondition children to the drum-like knocking sounds they will hear during the scan by having them listen to these sounds on earphones and also have them wear earplugs during the scan (average time 10 minutes) the children become comfortable with the procedure.

Brain-based learning research has given and will continue to give educational researchers neuroimaging data to help correlate classroom strategies to brain activity during the stages of learning. During the next decades, the neuroscience of learning will continue to provide data that neurocognitive researchers can use to develop and test classroom strategies for teaching the many components of reading.

What Research to Trust?

The increasing scientific knowledge about the physiology of how the human brain learns has the potential to significantly impact classroom instruction. For educators to take an informed leadership role on issues regarding the teaching of reading that are derived from brain research, we must understand the research, be able to evaluate the accuracy, credentials, and potential for bias in the so-called experts who interpret it, and find ways to develop and use strategies based on valid research to improve student success in reading.

The stated goal of much education legislation is for all students to learn to read. The goal of most educators extends beyond that—for students to learn not only the mechanics of reading and reading comprehension, but to also to develop a love of reading. The achievement of these goals begins when students receive instruction in the process of reading in a nonthreatening, engaging, and effective way. The best instruction comes from teachers who are qualified, informed, and have the support of administrators and curriculum responsive to the needs of all learners. With such support, individual classroom teachers still need to tweak their lessons to use the strategies or approaches that fit with their students' individual learning styles. Teachers can then provide a variety of motivating, personally relevant, and engaging reading strategies and materials such that reading becomes a choice and not a chore.

Most teachers are highly motivated to empower their students to become successful readers who take pleasure from the printed word. Some of the standardized testing that has resulted from partisan No Child Left Behind (NCLB) politization of education has made it more of a challenge for teachers to use differentiated techniques to best reach students with varied learning styles. With less time to plan, less flexibility inherent in some phonics-heavy reading instruction programs, and the increasing complexity and volume of brain research about reading, teachers don't often have the neuroscience background or time to independently evaluate the research or pseudoresearch presented in support of the reading curriculum programs they are required to use.

Peer-reviewed brain research can give solid biological data and explanations, but educators need to be cautious about what is claimed to be based on brain research and what is actually valid. For example, subsequent reevaluation of early PET scan research interpretations have given us reason to be cautious about which research is valid enough to connect with actual learning.

The first PET scan research to give information about brain development in children was part of a 1987 UCLA research project that was not intended to be an educational research tool. Doctors were evaluating the brain metabolism in patients with seizures and other neurological disorders impacting brain neural activity. This research studied 29 epileptic children ranging from 5 days of age through age 15. They first measured each child's resting metabolic brain state (metabolism of glucose when they were not stimulating the child with sensory or cognitive data). They determined that the highest rate of glucose metabolism during children's brain development studied (5 days to 15 years) was at age 3 or 4, when the metabolic rate was twice the glucose metabolism rate of adults. After age 4, the metabolism remained relatively unchanged until age 9 or 10, when it began to drop down to the adult range and leveled off by age 16 or 17 (Chugani, Phelps, & Mazziotta, 1987).

This 1987 UCLA brain development data was a side-product of the intention of the research to study the brain metabolism in children with seizures or other neurological diseases. It was not intended to be a tool for finding peak ages of brain metabolism and any correlation to times during which teaching interventions should be emphasized.

Problems arose when the brain metabolism information was assumed to imply more than it actually did. For example, there had been previous research where the density of synaptic connections between brain cells had been counted in brain samples from autopsy material in people of all ages (Epstein, 1978).

It turned out that there was correlation between the age when synaptic density (number of nerve to nerve connections or synapses) is greatest and the ages when glucose metabolism was greatest on the UCLA group's PET scans. However, neither of these findings proves that the *reason* for the greater metabolism is to maintain this greater density of synapses (connections between brain cells), nor that either synaptic density or brain metabolic activity is the direct cause of any potential for greater learning during those years (Chugani, 1996).

In fact, Chugani and his colleagues never claimed that periods of high metabolic activity were the optimal sensitive periods for learning to take place. That may turn out to be the case, but there still needs to be cognitive research tied to neuroimaging to make scientific claims about brain synaptic density, metabolic activity, and potential for greatest learning.

Neuroimaging for education and learning research is still largely suggestive, rather than completely empirical, in establishing a solid link between how the brain learns and how it metabolizes oxygen or glucose. Most of the strategies I will suggest are, to the best of my understanding of the brain, *compatible* with the research so far about how the brain seems to preferentially respond to the presentation of sensory stimuli. It would be premature and against my training as a medical doctor to claim that any of these strategies are as yet firmly validated by the complete meshing of simultaneous cognitive studies, neuroimaging, and educational classroom research. It is for now a combination of the art of teaching and the science of how the brain responds metabolically to stimuli that will guide educators in finding the best neuro-*logical* ways to present information to potentiate learning.

Evaluating the Brain Research for Reading

Evaluating the studies about what makes a good reader or what factors and strategies correlate with successful achievement of reading milestones can be tricky. Like the faulty logic that "correlates" milk drinking with murderers because 99 percent of all murderers drank milk regularly in childhood, the interest group that stands to gain when a curriculum is purchased or implemented can misrepresent data. Even with neuroimaging data there is disagreement about the interpretation of what scan results mean.

One such area of dispute is the *brain glitch theory* of reading difficulties that is based on faulty interpretation of brain imaging to prop up phonics-heavy curriculum. This theory proposes a specific site in the prefrontal cortex where a glitch or malfunction is the cause of many reading problems that can be corrected or improved by the phonics-heavy reading program incorporated in the NCLB-supported reading curriculum. The problem with the assertion that specific brain regions are the specific locations of defined parts of the complex reading process is that neuroimaging is not an exact science. Evidence from a study using magnetic stimulation tech-niques comparing phonological and semantic processing, in terms of specific areas of the prefrontal cortex activation, may suggest that there is significant evidence in favor of a segregation of phono-logical and semantic processing, but a number of questions would remain because neuroimaging can only demonstrate that brain activity is *correlated* with a cognitive task or process, but cannot demonstrate that the region *is necessary* for the task or process.

To make the assumption that the disruption of activity in a specific brain region is the cause of a reading glitch, there would need to be evidence of that precise reading difficulty when lesions occur in that designated part of the brain. Thus far, that type of evaluation using lesion studies has provided only mixed and not definitive evidence for the presence of precise, specific areas where a reading brain glitch is proposed to exist (Poldrack & Wagner, 2004).

Once neuroimaging has been used to evaluate brain activity before, during, and after reading interventions and those interven-tions are also quantified by comprehensive reading skill analysis, it may be possible to demonstrate objectively which reading interven-tion strategies are best for students based on which reading areas show abnormal metabolic activity on neuroimaging. That is not yet the case.

With these opportunities will also come the less scrupulous people who will prey on parents and educators using misleading interpretations of impressive, colorful PET scans or EEG brain maps as proof that their strategies are "brain-based" and therefore the best. Parents will come to their children's classroom and resource teachers seeking advice. Even with my background in neurology and education, I advise caution before signing up for programs that cost thousands of dollars and require multiple scans or brain maps to monitor progress.

To date, my analysis of the research does not reveal one program that conclusively and universally succeeds for all reading disorders. If there were, I believe that the outstanding academic curriculum and language arts specialists I have met would be recommending that program to school boards and parents. Because such programs are not yet confirmed by neuroimaging and supported by cognitive testing, I advise caution. I suggest that when parents ask about the latest brain-based research cures for dyslexia or other reading processing problems, the best advice is to have them consult with a district reading specialist who has no vested interest in outside private treatment programs. With that guidance, you can help save parents from expensive, time-consuming, commercial reading programs that prey on their guilt, pain, and love with colorful before and after brain scans that promise results they may not provide.

The good news is that the *direction* of well-controlled research is to seek evidence for brain changes following successful reading intervention strategies. My impression is that there will be suggestive findings that some of the students who overcome reading disabilities and demonstrate objective improvements on reading skill testing will have changes in their post-intervention brain scans. I believe that with more prospective neuroimaging and cognitive studies evidence will build that some interventions will correlate with improvements in specific reading skills and these students' neuroimaging will become more like the brain imaging scans of good readers. There may soon be a time when objective evidence will support specific strategies to improve faulty language processing networks. Until then, the strategies I use and will describe are what I interpret to be most compatible with the preliminary neuroimaging studies of the networks in the brain that appear most metabolically active during specific parts of the complex reading process.

1

From Syllable to Synapse: Prereading Through Decoding

To understand how students learn to read, we must first understand how the brain processes written information. The process of reading with comprehension appears to involve several essential and interrelated phases:

1. Information intake—focusing and attending to the pertinent environmental stimuli.

2. Fluency and vocabulary—associating the words on the page with stored knowledge to bring meaning to the text.

3. Patterning and networking—recognizing familiar patterns and encoding new information by linking it with prior knowledge.

Comprehension, retention, and use of information obtained through reading appear to be associated with prefrontal lobe activation and storage in neurons of the neocortex. The ultimate site where information gained from reading appears to be processed is in the frontal lobe's executive function centers. When comprehension and retention are successful, executive functioning appears to allow the information to be used to prioritize, plan, analyze, judge, and use the knowledge to make decisions that guide future actions.

After a discussion of mirror neuron research and prereading, there will follow my interpretation of the voluminous data accumulated through neuroimaging and EEG studies about the proposed brain reading systems. The purpose of this research summary and interpretation is not to artificially divide the brain's reading processing into discrete, independent reading pathways. Individual variation is very significant in reading, as it is in most neural activities. Data that has accumulated from neuroimaging studies while subjects are engaged in specific parts of the reading process are difficult to isolate. How do we know the subject is not using some internal visualization recognition rather than auditory recognition when they hear a sound not printed? We don't. Similarly, when subjects see a word, some may be internally verbalizing it while other subjects being scanned are automatically recognizing it as a familiar visual pattern. Given these uncontrollable factors, what I have tried to do with the reading pathway research is provide a general map of the most common brain pathways that appear to be activated in the complex, multistep process of reading. These pathways are generalizations and should not be interpreted as precise roadmaps.

Prereading

Even before children develop the ability to talk or read, their developing brains may be experiencing *imitation learning* through the activation of *mirror neurons.*

Giaccamo Rizzollati's 1996 discovery of what he named mirror neurons was part of his group's study of a cluster of neurons in the premotor cortex of the frontal lobes of monkeys (the region that corresponds to *Broca's area* in the cortex of the frontal lobe of humans—the brain center associated with the expressive and syntactic aspects of language). Rizzollati found that these brain cells fired when the monkeys performed specific actions with their hands such as picking up peanuts and putting them in their mouths. At first it was assumed that these neurons fired because they were sending messages to the hands to perform these motor activities (Rizzolatti, Fogassi, & Gallese, 2001). The researchers were surprised to discover that the mirror neurons that fired in the frontal lobe of a monkey when it picked up a peanut and ate it also fired when that monkey observed another monkey (or even the human researcher) performing the same activity. The theoretical correlation that followed was that the mirror neurons could allow the brain to not just "see" actions, emotions, or sensations, but also to respond to them by brain cell activations that mirror them. (Infants are not able to hold still for the several minutes required for accurate fMRI or other neuroimaging—so the theories of mirror images in very young children are speculative.) With respect to language development and other socializing behaviors, the mirror neurons may cause humans to experience internal representations of the body states they observe as if they were doing similar actions or experiencing similar emotions or sensations as another human they observe (Buccino et al., 2004).

In language this could mean that mirror neurons may build the foundation for babies to imitate, and perhaps later understand, the lip and tongue movements of others. This may be an explanation for the finding that when you stick your tongue out to some babies they imitate and stick out their tongues. The theory continues that after the mirroring of mouth and tongue movements could come the ability to mime vocalizations.

As mentioned previously, the strategies loosely based on pre-liminary interpretations of research such as mirror neurons remain theoretical. However, one area to watch for with respect to this research would be the opportunity to make early diagnosis of potential language problems in very young children at risk for speech and reading delays who may have abnormal responses in their mirror neurons to mimicry. For example, infant brain development is now becoming an area of investigation through EEG and laser eye tracking. In terms of early diagnosis, one study of thousands of babies "gaze-following" found that the skill appears first at about 10 to 11 months, and that babies who weren't proficient at gaze-following by the time they were 1 year old had much less advanced language skills at age 2 (Brooks & Meltzoff, 2005).

Another possibility with regard to mirror neuron research is that early and systematic priming (stimulating) of mirror neurons engaged in speech could be a strategy for building the preliminary building blocks of reading through stimulation of these mimicking neurons. This could potentially mean that modeling of verbal language with exaggerated lip and tongue movements, or exaggerating the sound and movement correspondence of labial sounds with graphemes on a page could have the prereading value of priming the mirror neurons. As babies become toddlers, concepts of print awareness such as left to right eye movements across a line of print, connecting words on a page to the lip movements of the reader, or even the actions of page turning could stimulate prereading mirror neurons.

Three Proposed Brain Systems and Pathways of Reading

Neuroimaging studies have implicated three interrelated systems that are the most active during parts of the reading process. One of these regions is in the frontal lobe and the other two are in posterior lobes—one posterior ventral (lower) and one posterior dorsal (higher).

The **frontal reading system** has been implicated in phonological processing and semantic processing (word analysis). This is also where Broca's area is found. Broca's area is involved in language processing, speech production, and comprehension. Neuron activation is increased in this area when words are spoken (Devlin, Matthews, & Rushworth, 2003).

The **ventral posterior processing system** (located in the occipital and temporal lobes) is most associated with orthographic processing (visual-phonological connections) of the pattern and form of words. This system is hypothesized to be the location of visual word pattern recognition because this region is activated when more experienced readers recognize whole words automatically.

However, this brain region is not purely a place of visual word rec-ognition, as it responds to any pronounceable printed letter string of both real and nonsense words (McCandliss, Cohen, & Dehaene, 2003).

Examination of the literature does *not* show a precise subpart of the left ventral occipital and temporal gyri that *consistently* shows abnormal neuroimaging in all subjects with underperformance in tasks of letter and word recognition. What appears valid is that some parts of these regions (also called the visual word form area, or VWFA) are the most active brain regions during the processing of orthographic-phonological connections.

This ventral posterior processing system is more activated in English-language readers than readers of Chinese and other lan-guages with complex characters. This difference may imply that the spelling-sound correspondence is more important for decoding English than it is for decoding Chinese, which uses characters that require more visual-spatial recognition (Siok, Perfetti, Jin, & Tan, 2004).

The **dorsal posterior reading system** encompasses parts of the parietal and temporal lobes, especially the angular, supramarginal and posterior superior temporal gyri. This system has been impli-cated in word analysis through the integration of visual features of printed words (visual-spatial recognition) rather than whole word recognition. This appears to be an area of the brain used by early readers when they analyze words by linking letters to sounds (Price, Moore, & Frackowiak, 1996).

In the future, brain reading research may offer additional com-parative data relative to the size of these response zones and the speed and order of information transmission from one brain area to another. As more data accumulates there will be the potential for more direct evidence concerning the instructional strategies most efficient for specific reading problems. Future neuroimaging may also provide techniques for earlier identification of students who need more support to achieve their optimal reading development.

The Neural Mechanisms of Phonemic Awareness

The ability to deal explicitly and segmentally with sound units smaller than the syllable (phonemes) has been researched with experimental and longitudinal studies in hopes of identifying the association between phonemic awareness and letter knowledge. This information could suggest which type of reading instruction is best suited to the early years of reading instruction. The importance of phonemic awareness in an alphabetic language such as English is in its relationship to beginning readers' perception of the differences between individual sounds in spoken words.

When comparing the brain scans of subjects during most activities, the location where the specific thinking processing takes place is roughly consistent from person to person. For example, the sensory processing area for smell is within a few millimeters of a specific location in the prefrontal lobe when subjects are tested with smells while in PET or fMRI scans. With regard to the general functions of producing verbal speech or recognizing familiar images, PET scans show that there is also fairly good consistency as to the size of the brain region dedicated to the activity in average readers.

Sensitivity to sound structure such as rhyme, alliteration, and segmentation is correlated with fMRI activity in the left superior temporal lobe and lower frontal lobe. These are the same brain areas in which brain metabolic activity appears to increase in direct relationship to phonological awareness. The early activity in these regions has been correlated with children's later reading achievement (Wagner et al., 1997). The fMRI evidence also suggests an order of the brain's phonological processing centers' maturation. The auditory response centers that respond earliest in the neurological development of reading are in these same phonological awareness regions of the left temporal lobe most associated with sound and hearing (Turkeltaub, Gareau, Flowers, Zeffiro, & Eden, 2003).

Neuroimaging also suggests correlations with the size of brain regions associated with specific cognitive activities, such as distinguishing the differences between sounds in spoken words. These variations in *response zone* size seem to be associated with the varied abilities some children have with respect to these specific reading skills. For example, when children are not aware of these differences in sounds, they appear to have more difficulty learning and applying the sound-letter correspondences needed to decode words (Eldridge, Engel, Zeineh, Bookheimer, & Knowlton, 2005).

New tools of brain research for reading are providing more detailed information about information transfer speed in the brain. Researchers have neuroelectric tools to shed light on the time-sensitive cognitive events that occur rapidly during such activities as word reading. To support theories of reading, a goal is to evaluate the timing of word reading events. For example, what is the brain doing during the 20 to 200 milliseconds before the eyes move from one word of text to the next?

Functional magnetic resonance imaging methods cannot provide information about such brief events, but to evaluate this type of temporal information there are now measurements available using *event-related potentials* (ERPs) and *magnetoencephalography* (MEG). These electrophysiological methods provide timelines for rapid events such as word identification that cannot be measured on neuroimaging. These time-location methods are complementary to space-location parameters in reading research. Studies of *rapid automatized naming* (RAN) of letters and objects is already demonstrating differences in reaction time in the posterior reading areas of students and may have predictive value for word reading skill development (Misra, Katzir, Wolf, & Poldrack, 2004).

With neuroimaging and neuroelectric data demonstrating the complexity and interdependency of the multiple brain regions that must all work successfully for students to develop reading skills, it is understandable that general intelligence is not always correlated with reading skills (Gardner, 1983). For example, a reduced number of neurons or delayed response of the neurons in a region of the brain dedicated to any of the parts of reading (phonemic awareness, visual perception, or phonological processing) may result in neural response or transmission problems that can result in reading difficulties without impacting any other areas of general intelligence (Nation & Snowling, 2004).

Based on some clinical studies, but not yet confirmed by neuroimaging or brain wave measurements, strategies for building phonemic awareness have included explicit instruction in sound-letter correspondence and phoneme manipulation (blending and segmenting) in phonics followed by repeated readings of fully decodable text comprised of letter-sound pairs already learned (Santa & Hoien, 1999). Other approaches favor more implicit connection of sound-letter correspondences using whole language activities that are associated with higher student interest and therefore attentive focus (Foorman, 1995). As neuroimaging scans and brain wave speed measurement (qEEG) improve in accuracy it may be possible to determine which of these strategies or combination of strategies will produce the best results in phonemic awareness instruction and practice.

Phonological Processing

Listening to and understanding speech and reading the written word both involve identifying the individual sounds that make up words. The process of recognizing those phonemes and subsequently identifying the words that they combine to make is called phonological processing.

In spoken language, phonological processing takes place automatically at a preconscious, instinctual level. This process automatically allows us to put phenomes together to say words and to deconstruct the words into phonemes to understand spoken language. Unlike speech, reading requires the understanding that written words are composed of letters of the alphabet that are intentionally and conventionally related to segments of spoken words (alphabetic principle).

The alphabet and letter-sound correspondence is an artificial construct that gives speech concrete representation at the phonological level. Therefore, unlike automatic speech production and comprehension, reading must be learned on a conscious level. Children need to learn the phonological processing of reading and recognize that specific sequences of letters represent the phonological structure of words (orthography).

Functional MRI scanning has demonstrated brain-processing regions that are particularly active in phonological processing. Phonological processing of grapheme-phoneme connections is associated with activation in the dorsal posterior reading system where early readers analyze words by linking letters to sounds (Price, Moore, & Frackowiak, 1996).

A key area of the dorsal posterior system, the *angular gyrus*, was significantly more active in letter naming compared with object naming. This may be an area of research that could lead to more specific strategies to develop this brain region (Thierry, Boulanouar, Kherif, Ranjeva, & Demonte, 1999).

Activities That Build Phonemic Awareness

The strategies I will describe for increasing phonemic awareness and other aspects of reading development are drawn from my own scientific interpretations of the research and the practices that have been successful in my classroom, or that I observed in the classrooms of others. If the strategy is one I learned or read about and then observed I give credit to the originator. If the strategy is one that is in such wide use that the originator is not formally acknowledged in the research I reviewed there may be no credit given. Most of the strategies are in that category—techniques in general use that I have modified to conform to the best supported, well-conducted brain based research using neuroimaging, neuroelectric measurements, and cognitive measurements.

Consider telling students your reasons for these activities so they understand why they are participating in what might otherwise seem to be, at best, games and, at worst, boring or confusing drills. When I have given short explanations about how the activity they will do will change their brains, students enjoy the information about their own brains. This may be because children learning to read are at the egocentric ages when the idea of learning about themselves resonates with their interest. They also appreciate being told the reasons behind the activities because they feel they are working with me on a team. One 2nd grade student said, "I like it better when I know why you want us to do something, especially if it is something that is not too much fun." His classmate added, "When teachers tell us why we have to know something and why it is good for us it doesn't make it easier, but it makes me want to do it more."

One activity is segmenting sounds and then blending them together using both real words and nonsense words. This activity gives students practice manipulating phenomes and is consistent with the research supporting stimulation of both posterior processing systems (McCandliss, Cohen, & Dehaene, 2003).

Another activity is oral blending and segmenting paired with letters. This process may help students practice the alphabetic principle (the establishment of a correspondence between a phoneme and a written symbol). Here is an example of segmenting: "Say the first sound in 'run,' then say each sound separately. Say the word without the /n/ sound. Say 'run' without the /r/ sound." An example of blending would be: "Say 'ap'. Put /n/ in front of 'ap' and say the new word, 'nap.'" Using individual blackboards or dry-erase boards with teacher modeling on a large dry-erase board makes blending and segmenting a fun writing/reading activity. Body or hand movements make auditory tasks more visible and have the potential to stimulate multiple sensory intake areas for greater memory and connection to learning style preference (especially for kinesthetic learners). For example, after first modeling the activity, ask students to open/close hands or take a step forward or backward when they hear individual sounds in words you say as you put vocal emphasis on the phonemes.

Many of the strategies for success at all stages of reading have been used by teachers for decades. The ones I will emphasize and describe in more detail in later chapters are the strategies that now appear best supported by well-designed, brain-based research using the newer neuroimaging and neuroelectric monitoring technology.

The fact that individual students develop and coordinate the many skills involved in reading at different rates and in different ways makes it challenging for teachers to structure lessons that benefit the individual needs and reading developmental levels of all students. Fortunately, the future of brain research interpretation is likely to provide more strategies to help educators assess students' developmental readiness and neurological strengths and challenges.

2

Patterning Strategies

....

The brain naturally works to find patterns, make sense of information and experiences, and evaluate the personal and emotional significance of incoming data (Coward, 1990). Effective reading instruction that corresponds to the brain's patterning processes results in more successful and efficient learning. Recognizing that a particular stimulus fits into an established category appears to be the most efficient way for the brain to learn new information. For example, neural scans show metabolic activity in the prefrontal and hippocampal regions when the brain recognizes new words as belonging to a previously created category. When the word the subjects see does not stimulate any associated memory or category link, their brain scans fail to show this activation in their memory processing regions (Coward, 1990).

The brain receives information through the senses, and not all sensory input is equally valuable. The brain must sort the input and focus attention on the information it determines to be most valuable at the moment. If students cannot see the patterns in letters, words, or sentences, they are less likely to link new information with pre-existing information. Without the organization provided by patterning, they may not successfully direct information to the executive functioning frontal lobe brain regions where working memories appear to be paired with existing data and coded into relational long-term memories that can advance reading skills.

Pattern Recognition Reading Research

A recent study showed fMRI evidence indicating that reading acquisition begins with rote pattern recognition of words based on visual features or context (Turkeltaub et al., 2003). For example, a young child might recognize the word "yellow" because it has two tall lines in the middle, and might only recognize the word "stop" when it appears on a red octagonal sign. As children attain alphabetic knowledge, they learn phoneme-to-grapheme correspondence and use phonetic cues to decode words. As reading skills mature, readers appear to consolidate commonly occurring letter sequences, such as "tion," into clusters and process these clusters as units, allowing them to identify unknown words by analogy to words they already know (Turkeltaub et al., 2003).

Pattern Recognition Strategies

Pattern construction and pattern recognition are integral to learning to read, from the time children first use the alphabetic principle to identify printed words. Patterning is the process by which words are identified by linking the abstract representations in letters (graphemes) to the sounds of the words. Mastering pattern recognition requires persistent practice, especially by students who do not pick up patterns readily. Just as neuroimaging reveals that learning to read is not just one process isolated to a single brain center, teaching students to read also involves multiple and varied types of classroom activities that need to be modeled, practiced, and monitored with ongoing feedback for successful coding of information into patterns and storing of these patterns into larger patterns or categories.

To complicate the already complex progression of learning to read for the "average" student, there are individual variations in students' abilities to recognize patterns or to code data into patterns the brain can process. Students enter school with different literacy backgrounds and predispositions for reading. Even before patterning instruction begins, a process of screening and continuous assessment needs to be set in place to guide decisions about grouping, the pace of instruction, and needed instruction adaptations. Patterning evaluations include assessments of students' abilities to segment words, blend sounds, and categorize new information into patterns.

For example, some students cannot sort items by color, shape, or size. These students face recognition problems even in the initial process of letter or word identification. Other students have structural or functional defects in their brain that inhibit processing of visual input. Their brains don't adequately encode new information into patterns that can be transported through the neural networks of short-term memory into long-term memory (Coward, 1990). Strategies are needed that support and compensate for the range of responses that take place in individual brains as students respond differently to words on a page.

Successful patterning is reinforced in reading when teachers help students create brain-recognizable patterns out of the information they need to learn. This can be facilitated by presenting material using organized, engaging, well-sequenced activities that allow students to recognize patterns in a meaningful way (Nummela & Rosengren, 1986).

When early readers are beginning to learn nouns, starting with objects, people, and places, model how they can use visual patterning to visualize and then draw pictures of these words to develop mental patterns they can associate with these common nouns when they read them independently (Coward, 1990). Visual art activities such as drawing develop spatial reasoning skills and may increase students' ability to create abstractions and visualize the images that words represent as they learn to read (Wesson, 2006). Have prereaders and early readers draw the visual images that come to mind when you read books aloud. They can share these with classmates or they can be posted on walls. Drawing pictures coincides with the brain's natural inclination to look for patterns, sequence, and order.

Strategies That Correlate Phonemes with the Brain's Patterning Systems

Recognition of sounds, letters, and letter-sound correspondences are the primary language patterns fundamental to developing word recognition skills. To help students develop their skills at recognizing the underlying separate sound elements that are the essential categories or patterns of spoken language, they can practice constructing patterns from these separate sound elements.

As described in the previous chapter, activities that emphasize phonemes and segmenting words orally and later in writing can help students hear the component sounds and recognize categories of sounds. When they then blend these sounds, first by repetition and then by experimenting with new patterns themselves, they are establishing categories. The goal of these patterning strategies is to help students recognize the patterns and connections between the more than 40 speech sounds and the more than 100 spellings that represent them. As they become more familiar with the patterns, students can build brain familiarity and circuitry to achieve the goal of identifying phonemes and words automatically and thereby build their abilities to decode unknown words.

Demonstrate Word Patterns

Provide repetitive input of information in an enjoyable context to maintain student motivation and to encourage children to build consistent patterns. This repetition should build and reinforce the neuronal activation that appears to correlate to the brain's response to sensory input (Tallal, Merzenich, Jenkins, & Miller, 1999). Use a variety of visual activities to emphasize patterns in word families, spelling patterns, prefixes, suffixes, and word roots. For example, to help students recognize the repeating patterns in words (hiber-**nate**, deco**rate**, collabo**rate**), make these patterns more obvious by emphasizing the repeating parts of the words with different colors on a whiteboard or blackboard, with different fonts on PowerPoint presentations or on computer screens, or by using color, highlighting, or bold print in printed material. Auditory patterns can be emphasized by voice pitch, slow speed, robotic speech, or volume emphasis. When students are repeating spoken words with patterns they should be encouraged to respond with similar emphasis. (This activity has appealed especially to my students with interpersonal, active, kinesthetic learning styles.)

These same patterns can be emphasized by modeling physical movements that correspond to the phoneme or sound pattern to be learned. In my classroom I have had students stand and, like high tech cyborgs, rotate 90 degrees each time I say a distinct word sound ("buh" "ah" "tuh" in "bat") or when I verbalize each syllable of a word we are segmenting. This activity can be especially useful after a period of sitting still, when the movement is a form of brain break and can stimulate additional motor-responsive neuronal tracts. (These brain breaks, and other destressors, will be described further in Chapter 4). Later, as grammar and punctuation are studied, I use many of these same pattern highlighting strategies (font, color, size) to emphasize recurring patterns for punctuation rules such as commas in sequence or spelling rules such as *ei* and *ie* order in words like re**cei**ve and bel**ie**ve.

Have Students Manipulate Phoneme Patterns

As with most practice activities, patterning activities are more meaningful and engaging to students when they manipulate the information themselves. As children are helped to recognize patterns, such as words being composed of letter patterns that are represented in the sounds of spoken words, they are learning in a manner consistent with the way the brain is currently interpreted to work through pattern recognition and construction. One activity that will help students with phonemic awareness is to give students index cards with words that can be combined into compound words. They walk around the class (providing kinetic activity and a brain break) and find classmates with cards that work with their own cards to form compound words. Each time they find a new compound word match, the students add it to the growing list on the board.

Why Manipulating Patterns Helps the Brain Do Its Job

Seeing or hearing patterns may help students learn by activating the brain's recognition systems so new data can be recognized, categorized, and stored in the patterned format that is compatible with neuronal transport and storage of information.

If each pattern that the brain discovers can be added to the learner's information storage categories, it makes sense to me to use strategies to help students make permanent memories of the patterns so their future recognition will be automatic. When students then manipulate patterns by building on them, changing them, and even playing with them, the patterns can have greater likelihood of being stored in permanent memory. The goal is to use strategies that help students practice finding patterns so new information can be coded and matched with existing related patterned brain material. Consider ways to organize and present material to encompass students' patterning systems to help them create these meaningful and relevant connections with existing patterns.

Categories as Patterns

Moving Objects into Categories

Start with obvious categories such as a collection of pictures, small plastic animals, or toy vehicles, and have students work in pairs to sort them into categories and then name the categories. What characteristic of the items did they use to put them into a grouping together? Next, place three items that are in the same category with one that does not belong and have students select the one that does not belong and explain why. This can even be done using small plastic objects on the overhead projector. When students are proficient with these more obvious categories, move to shapes, which also work well on overhead projectors, followed by partner pair practice.

When the class is ready for a more kinesthetic activity, you can teach the students a game where one student selects an undisclosed pattern or category (such as class members wearing sneakers, something green, long/short pants, long/short sleeve shirts, etc.) and calls the students who fit in the category to the front of the room one by one until observing classmates recognize the commonality.

Being proficient at pattern-finding and recognizing rules benefits from many experiences with patterns. Follow-up homework could be to have a treasure hunt at home or with parents in the park making (or sketching) items that are in the same category. These could then become bulletin board displays with the names of the categories covered with a flip-up card so classmates can challenge themselves to name the categories.

Patterning skills can be developed by activities where children file or match material systematically using objects or cards with names of objects written on them. They could do this in pairs or at workstations by matching names with familiar faces or foods into categories (fruit, vegetable, meats). These pair matching activities can be reinforced with input of additional learning senses. Children can say the names of pairs aloud, write them down, or diagram them. This can be done at a learning center in their notebooks or on work progress cards you review for assessment and feedback.

Pattern recognition activities can also be embedded in games. For example, students can play a modified game of *Jeopardy* by answering questions to which the answers are words that demonstrate the pattern being learned.

Creating Their Own Categories

Because readers are not automatically given category cues when they need to identify new words, it could increase word identification efficiency if students develop more than one category system for storing data about the same objects or words. For example the word "drum" if learned by seeing the word (visual input), hearing the word (auditory input), and tapping their hands on their desks as if playing drums (tactile-kinesthetic input) could be stored in memory categories related to each of these sensory inputs. This redundancy could help speed the identification of the word subsequently because more than one receiving center would be available as relational categories to recognize and categorize the word when it is seen again.

Students appear to use a different kind of thinking when they create original patterns following rules they create (Grabowski, Damasio, & Damasio, 1998). Activities that engage students in building categories can start as early as preschool. Building category practice can be done with a bag of mixed buttons. After first modeling the procedure, you can have students work on their own or in pairs to sketch the categories they discover. This would also work as a language arts learning center activity. With a bag of buttons, students can decide multiple ways to categorize them. Students are likely to start with more obvious classifications such as size or color, but with prompting they will move to other patterns such as two or four holes, or smooth or indented. Ask verbally, or on cards at learning stations, leading questions such as, "How else can you group the buttons by other similarities?" or "What else do some of the buttons have in common?"

Stimulate Use of Learned Patterns

Once the students have been engaged and their brains' pattern recognition systems have been activated by a review or new strategy such as highlighting or underlining to emphasize the pattern they have learned, you can support the pattern by connecting it to activities where they use it. This mental manipulation could build and reinforce the brain networks of connecting neurons and dendrites and increase the permanence and speed of accessibility to the stored pattern so it can be used to process future input.

Word recognition can be compatible with the brain's patterning systems when modeling and practicing activities emphasize the pattern. Strategies that practice patterning words and letters into categories could increase students' ability to recognize and file new data into existing classifications quickly and accurately. The assumption is that if words are taught in relation to existing categories they will be more efficiently recognized in specific regions where the brain stores related data. That process would logically be faster and more efficient than a whole-brain random search when the new data is not recognized as belonging to any existing stored, related pattern.

Strengthen Neuron Networks

Strategies That Reinforce Learned Patterns

Because the brain cross-references information in multiple categories and each sensory input has its own reception and memory storage station, it makes sense that reviewing patterns with different sensory experiences could make it easier for students to access the patterns. An example of multisensory input would be to use sound, color, movement, or touch to provide input to multiple senses. For example, start by using a color to highlight the "ate" word ending (keep the rest of the word in black type). Or, when the pattern is reinforced in a review session, use a different verbal emphasis on the common word ending (volume, speed, or pitch) to connect it with another brain storage area (auditory). Use graphic organizers to reinforce the learned pattern, such as a flagpole sketch with banners hanging to the left. The flagpole is labeled "ate" and the banners hanging on its left side would be filled in with beginnings of words that end in "ate." Students draw sketches representing several action verbs ending with "ate" such as *concentrate*, *celebrate*, and *decorate*.

Another activity would be to give worksheets to students with the instructions that they can stop the specific practice activity after they achieve a certain number of correct answers in a row. For example if they match root words correctly with the "ate" suffix five times in a row they can move on to the next level. After students reach their individual initial mastery points they continue with a choice of activities that involve using the newly learned patterning skill at a higher cognitive level, such as using words ending in "ate" to creating a story or write a letter. By individualizing practice options after one level of mastery is attained, the students will all remain engaged during the practice time and work in their appropriate zone of proximal development (ZPD).

Separating Similar Meanings from Categories

Once students are comfortable with putting things or abstractions into categories based on similarities, the next step is to have them distinguish between items that share *categories* from those that share similar *meanings*. For example "run" and "walk" are both in the category of movement and "walk" and "stroll" have shared meaning with respect to speed. The goal is to build higher cognitive categorizing skills and hopefully stimulate more patterning neural networks by having them analyze groups of words for the type of pattern they represent.

Category and Meaning Activity

This activity asks students to practice grouping words by either category or meaning. It starts with modeling, moves to whole class practice, and concludes with pairs or small groups making their own questions and quizzing their neighboring groups. I start the activity with a group discussion of categories. I ask them to give me examples of categories in general, such as types of foods, sports equipment, things found in a classroom, parts of a cow. Students add other categories and I select several for them to give examples for. "What could you put in the category of sports equipment?"

The process is repeated for words with similar meanings and, depending on the age group, I may remind students of the term "synonym." I start with nouns that I explain have similar meanings to other words. For younger students I would use words such as "dog, canine, hound, and pooch," and for older students I would use verbs such as "hurl, propel, throw, fling." When I think that students are ready for guided peer work, I offer grade-appropriate practice pages for students to work on with partners.

I use the following prompt: "Look at this group of words (or pictures for younger students) and write (or make a check by) the word 'category' if they are all in a category or classification. If you think they have similar meanings write or check 'similar meaning.'" Sample questions and answers:

Frightened/sad/happy/embarrassed: Classification category (emotions)

Blouse/pants/socks/jacket: Classification category (clothes)

Little/small/petite/miniature: Similar meaning

Sharp/pointed/prickly/spiky: Similar meaning

After assessing student work and giving corrective feedback and additional examples to reinforce the learning the following day, I have students create their own word groups of similar meanings and similar categories. I motivate them by telling them that I will select some of the word groups to be given as practice in the next lesson. If students do not get a word group quite right I can give them positive reinforcement and corrective feedback when I return their proposed sample questions to them showing how I modified them so they could be used in the class practice lists. For example if a pair writes "snow/rain/hail/rainbow" I change it to "snow/rain/hail/sleet and ask them why they think I substituted "sleet" for "rainbow." The students are receptive to this corrective feedback because they have already received the positive reinforcement of having their grouping selected, even if it has been slightly altered. Having the student-generated word groupings from which to prepare the class worksheet lets me make assessments of their understanding as I check and modify the groupings for accuracy.

In addition, I am able to sort the groupings by levels of complexity. I start the class worksheet with the easier groupings and increase to the more complex ones. With that organization students can progress to their own ability levels and the results of individual student work on the class worksheet gives me additional assessment information. Sample groupings created by students:

Hot/burning/steaming/boiling: Similar meaning

Huge/large/giant/big: Similar meaning

Sun/moon/stars/comets: Category (things in our solar system)

Paw/snout/tail/ears: Category (parts of a dog)

Patterning and Vocabulary

Words are fundamentally conceptual—although they are physical objects, they represent something ideational. Just giving students definitions of words or having them evaluate the context of word use does not fully use the brain's patterning style of identifying information. The value of word pattern sorting extends beyond their definition to relating words to the pattern of categorization where they fit. Students attend to how words relate to other words through a number of types of categories such as similar meaning, shared classification category, semantic grouping, root similarities, and word beginnings and endings.

After discussing a word like "metamorphosis," students can use graphic organizers to place the word in multiple categories and to add other words to each category.

• Words endings: other words ending in "sis" such as photosynthesis, analysis, phagocytosis, and mitosis.

• Words with similar meanings: change, transformation, and alteration.

• Words with similar roots: morph, morphology, amorphous, and morpheme.

• Words with similar prefixes: metaphor, metaphysical, and metacognition.

Students can work in groups and use dictionaries to find other words for each category and to talk about how the words in each category relate and differ.

This activity is particularly useful for scientific vocabulary and other subject-specific vocabulary. Strategies to facilitate scientific vocabulary acquisition become increasingly critical in high school—the number of new words encountered in a high school biology book exceeds the number of words encountered in two years of foreign language instruction (Drew, 1996).

Further word analysis and patterning in science can include comparison of the word through its scientific form, common use form, and even its companion word in another language. An example is the word "infirm," which is "sick" in everyday language and "infermo" in Spanish. This helps bring in students who have English as their second language. Analysis of scientific terms also demonstrates the value of formal scientific terminology because it is more specific or precise to use the word "botanist" instead of saying "someone who studies plants."

After I give students a list of science vocabulary words pertinent to their unit of study, I ask volunteers to offer less formal synonyms for the words. I list the scientific words on the board, such as genetics, mitosis, heredity, recessive, and chromosome. Students have already had some exposure to the words so students with familiarity with the words are willing to volunteer other words to substitute for the scientific terms. What the class realizes is that it usually takes several words to convey the meaning of the single scientific term. This leads to a discussion of the value of scientific vocabulary with the goal of increasing their motivation for learning these words because they recognize their value.

Student responses include
- "Scientific terminology lets us be more precise."
- "Scientific words have logic and fit together in a way that makes sense and makes communication with other scientists comprehensible and logical."

Pattern Manipulation Stimulates Brain Plasticity

The next brain patterning process in reading is to promote long-term memory of the new information through its manipulation (active cognitive processing) or by using the information to make some judgment, connection, analysis, perform an activity, etc. To increase successful pattern manipulation I provide students with multisensory opportunities to act on and process the newly acquired patterned information through executive function. This manipulation appears to help newly learned information go from working memory to long-term memory storage where it may physically change the brain's networks by building new dendrites, synaptic connections, and relational memory links. This is associated with the fascinating process of *brain plasticity.*

Brain Plasticity

Before neuroimaging, most neuroscientists believed that only young brains were plastic (changeable). It was believed that the connections between the brain's neurons developed in the first few years of childhood and then became permanent. The neural research of the past decades has revealed that human brains are *plastic* in that they can change in both growth and reduction of the nerve fibers that connect neurons to one another (dendrites) in response to learning and conscious manipulation of information (practice can promote growth) or from neglect of stimulation (cellular shrinkage and death).

With respect to language, this conscious manipulation is believed to include responding to the information we hear or read by using it for activities, visualizing it, discussing it, or writing about it. It is this use of new information in some "thinking" or acting process that activates higher executive cognitive function, such as making a choice, prediction, or decision based on the information. Plasticity research associates this mental processing of information with building the new neural circuits of neurons and their connecting fibers that are associated with increased long-term memory (Wagner et al., 1997).

With the goal of increasing memory and retention, reading research using brain imaging suggests that increased brain stimulation could result in greater memory and retention. This appears to be true from the basics of reading through decoding and the building of reading comprehension skills. The strategies I have modified and developed in response to this plasticity research are planned to offer multisensory, engaging, and thought-provoking lessons followed by individualized opportunities to verbalize, write, or create something using a new language arts skill or new information students read in hopes of building more connecting dendrites. The object of this growth of more neural connections is to increase the efficiency and speed of information transit through memory processing, category matching, patterning, storage, and recall. The strategies I use are aimed at offering students more opportunities to receive, pattern, and consciously manipulate new information.

The mental manipulation I strive to incorporate into planning lessons is to include activities and discussions where students actively "think" about the information with problem solving, analysis, comparison/contrast, creating graphic organizers, and other appropriately challenging higher cognitive processing.

Prediction and Preview to Create Patterns

Children's brains already have categories based on background, previous knowledge, and past experience. When new information fits with a patterning system and an existing category, the brain can automatically sort it into compatible patterns to fit into these categories. Strategies such as previewing the text, or asking students to make predictions or think about what they would do if they were the characters in the book provide templates that can be used to pattern incoming information for greater comprehension and connection with prior knowledge.

Previewing can be part of planning a reading activity. When students look ahead and foresee a likely outcome for a project or paper, or a vocabulary or grammar assignment, they can use their foresight and metacognition from previous similar experiences to prepare for potential challenges.

Patterning Through a Predicting, Planning, and Modifying Activity

For this engaging activity suitable for upper elementary through high school students, I model how students can predict, anticipate, and modify plans for a long-term assignment involving a thematic unit based on information students acquire through reading. I give the example of using prediction, anticipation of needs, and plan modification with respect to a fun activity such as planning a trip to a foreign country. I will take you through the steps of this activity:

1. Each student selects a country of personal interest. Students make *predictions* about a proposed visit to that country. I ask them to think about what kind of clothing and currency they'll need, how they'll get around, what language or languages they'll be communicating in, what places they'll want to visit, and so on.

2. I ask them to add a few of their own categories. This requires them to *anticipate* individual needs based on their individual interests. For example, if they are interested in scuba diving in Australia, what additional supplies, certifications, and information will they need?

3. We spend a few hours using library books and the Internet to see if their predictions were correct and to make the *modifications* needed. For example was it correct to predict that a scuba trip to Australia required a visa, or did they need just a passport? Was American currency easily accepted in Australia or would they need to exchange currency? Would the weather be the same as here in their planned trip time during their July summer vacation, or would that be winter weather in Australia? Finding out

information from books after predicting makes the investigation more goal-directed and the information obtained more meaningful to the individual. They are motivated by the country and activity of their choice and more alert to see if their predictions were correct.

4. We discuss how their imaginary trips would have been more successful and enjoyable because they predicted, anticipated, and modified as they read information about their destinations. Students have commented, "Predicting and looking helped me slow down to focus on important things." "At first I was impulsive and just thought about the foods I'd eat and the places I'd visit in Rome. After predicting, anticipating, and modifying I realized I had left important things out. If I do take a trip I'll be thoughtful rather than impulsive." Those insights came from students ages 11 and 12!

Because patterning is the brain's way of coding, storing, connecting, and retrieving information, students at any age can benefit from patterning activities. Patterning for the youngest students can start out with sorting. As students are developing reading comprehension skills, additional patterning skills are needed to retrieve stored information and activate new connections to successfully consolidate new and prior knowledge.

Story Prediction Activity

Give students written prediction papers to complete after they have explored a new book for the first time. After a class discussion of what they might expect after examining the cover, the table of contents, the illustrations, and perhaps the first paragraph, they fill out the prediction questions. (An accommodation here for ELL or LD students is to have them preread or have someone preread the first chapter or paragraph to them before the class discussion.) Sample Questions: When is the story taking place? Who are the main characters? What problems could arise? Who seems (fill in the adjective that is age and book appropriate) nice, honest, loyal, friendly, mean?

After making their predictions, students will be invested in seeing if their predictions were correct. To add more motivation, have students discuss their predictions with a partner and give their reasons. After a few chapters or pages, depending on grade level, when there is evidence of a problem for one or more characters ask students what they would do in the character's place. This makes it more likely that their brains will read with a purpose. They may be motivated to pattern and categorize input because they are now involved in personally meaningful problem-solving activities. The input can now be sorted into categories they pattern with the goal of collecting data that supports their predictions and their personal ideas about what the character should do. Graphic organizers can be helpful. As students read or hear information from text that contradicts their prediction they can have brain practice sorting fact from opinion or prediction from actuality.

The following patterning activities are ones I have used successfully with the goal of stimulating and exercising students' executive function and patterning networks. I have based these strategies on modifications of activities that educators have used in classrooms for decades. My modifications are to increase patterning with interactive discussions, charts, and graphic organizers, and to add relevance and personal interest by including information about how their own brains work. These adapted strategies, such as the following KWL activity, are based on my interpretation of the research described previously—that stimulating brain networks appears to increase their efficiency and capacity.

The familiar KWL activity can be used in the introduction of a new literacy technique or strategy to stimulate prior knowledge and student engagement. For students to feel comfortable to participate freely it is sometimes helpful to emphasize the "What I *think* I know" aspect of this discussion. I write on the overhead, board, or class list *any* information suggested by a student, even if it is not correct, while making it clear that the list is of suggestions and opinions, not facts, until the topic is investigated further and the class revisits the opinions when we complete the "*What I learned*" final list. (KWL adapted from Ogle, 1986.)

For a KWL activity about camouflage, I start by explaining, "We will investigate animal camouflage and use our brain patterning powers while we make a class chart of predictions before our investigation. First think about the *Where's Waldo* book we read and consider why Waldo was hard to find." (For younger students we have a class discussion about this before seeing the animal video or pictures to give them a base or category upon which to build the data they will be receiving about camouflage.) Think about the video we watched of animals camouflaged in their habitats. (You can show a nature video or pictures.)"Now, on this chart we will be listing ideas we have that are our opinions about what we think we know about animal camouflage. You don't have to be positive that your idea is a true fact. That is what we'll find out as we learn more. Just share things you think you know."

At this point I remind the students about our community policy of not interrupting or correcting classmates when we are sharing opinions or personal beliefs. Depending on the age or class I might give some examples: "If I say that I think camouflage in animals is when they put on army camouflage jackets to hide from other animals to play paintball, would you raise you hand and say that I'm wrong or being silly?" If students don't respond I answer myself, "Of course you wouldn't because in our class we respect each other's right to offer opinions as long as they are not hurtful." I continue, "Will you have a chance to use the factual information you already know and the additional knowledge we learn to later go back over this list of what we think we know and make corrections?" Again, if there is no student response, I answer myself, "Yes you will, so keep notes to remind yourself about things on this list you want to discuss later."

After we complete the "K" part of the KWL chart we continue to the "W" section listing the things we "Want to Know" about camouflage. This is an opportunity to increase student engagement by lowering the affective filters because there is not the stress of saying something "wrong" and feeling embarrassed. It helps that the class community has learned that asking questions is something I respect and appreciate (as long as the question hasn't just been asked and answered while the student was not paying attention). This is also an opportunity to build interest because when students see their questions written on a class list they seem to build intrinsic motivation to stay goal directed to find the answers. This all relates back to patterning and executive functioning as students are practicing prioritizing, predicting, judgment, and analysis as they see the categories written down on the KWL list. Using graphic organizers such as KWL lists give students' brains exposure to external patterning, just as sorting of buttons did when they were younger.

Sample student questions for the "W" list I have been excited about are listed here. These questions delighted me because I could perceive that students were thinking in patterns and categories and using relational memory.

• "Do predators and prey both use camouflage and do they use the same types of camouflage?"

• "Is camouflage one of the animal adaptations we studied like the way animals evolved to get food when their food supplies changed?"

• "Do people use camouflage in other ways, not just to hide in battles or hunting? I mean does camouflage get used in art or by scientists when they want to watch animals?"

• "Is using makeup, like in a play, camouflage?"

• "I see the word 'flag' in camouflage. Is that a root or suffix?"

After we complete the "W" part of the KWL chart and begin whole class or small group ability-level reading, students are encouraged to take notes as they learn facts they want to add to the "What I learned" part of the chart. When students take these notes rather than call out the information immediately, they are building their executive function of planning as they build relational memory patterning skills.

My take on the research is that this is a process of individual discovery of information. Students are goal-focused on finding information in the reading. When putting the information into their own written words follows their discovery of the information they seek, there is a greater probability of connecting with their prior knowledge as their thinking, analysis, and judgment processes of executive function are activated. This could be the step that moves information from short- to long-term memory.

Lesson Considerations: You could have younger students raise their hands during the teacher reading or read-around when they hear or read a fact for the "L" column and to say one or two words for you to write down on a temporary list. These cues would be used at the conclusion of the reading to prompt the students to give the more complete information they want to have listed on the "L" chart. Limiting students to a few words won't interrupt the flow of the reading. Also, the younger the students, the more frequently the reading should be stopped to allow for these additions to the "L" list before the information leaves their short-term memories.

Using Computers to Build Patterning Skills

Even when teachers do their best to use a balanced whole-brain approach to teaching pattern recognition and construction, some children need additional practice and more individualized review and reinforcement. Small reading groups help meet individual needs, but computer assisted lessons can help differentiate instruction so that students who need more support will get it, while other students will be challenged at their own levels.

What to Look For in Computer Reading and Patterning Programs

• **Flexibility and individualization** are the attributes of computer programs best suited to the complexity and diversity of students' reading progress. Printed text requires students to try to fit themselves to the specific pattern of the print (size, font, color), whereas computer flexibility can offer options such as turning pages through clicks rather than motor manipulation of paper, using the keyboard or mouse to highlight patterns (e.g., seeing words sequentially highlighted can support left-to-right tracking), or enlarging or color-coding the sections of text they need to focus on. Certainly the goal is for all students to be able to respond to all the types of text they will encounter during a lifetime of reading. Nevertheless, for struggling readers or students needing more scaffolding as they build fluency and patterning skills, computers can offer the manipulation of text to best suit their learning style strengths and most responsive neural receptors in their brains' reading networks. Once the students master the reading skill using the pattern manipulations to facilitate their success, the scaffolding can be gradually reduced as their brains become more receptive to the sensory input of text that is not enhanced through computer manipulation.

• **Monitoring:** The best computer programs are able to keep track of individual student progress and continue assessment and appropriate repetition until mastery is attained. Look for software that lets you monitor students' time spent, progress, and learning speed, and see not only the concepts they have mastered, but also the concepts that are in their ZPD (Greenlee-Moore & Smith, 1996).

• **Periodic Reassessments:** Look for a system where periodic assessments review all the skills practiced in the program. This can reinforce stored memory while prompting review sessions when knowledge gaps are revealed.

- **Interaction:** The interactive quality of computer reading programs can help engage, motivate, guide, and support students with activities that are both surprising and controllable. Programs are available that enable students to write, draw and animate pictures to match with text, ask a word or letter to say its own name, have a story read, see the lyrics to a song while listening to it, or record their own voices to accompany their own text or pictures.
- **Feedback:** Student feedback can be a tool to reinforce neuronal circuits in the brain. Look for programs that give positive as well as clear corrective feedback. The positive feedback can be in graphic illustrations of the amount of material mastered, auditory praise, pleasing sounds, or points. One website my students enjoy in math shows a picture of a ferris wheel (www.walter-fendt.de/m11e/conversion.htm). Each correct answer lights a seat on the ferris wheel and when they are all filled the wheel rotates around several times and carousel music is played. The positive feedback is successful when students feel acknowledged for their accomplishments in the learning and mastery they achieve. This is the type of response I look for in strategies that are compatible with the theories described in detail in Chapter 4 about the dopamine-reward system.

Because the reading software is continuously improving, it may be useful to consult your reading, curriculum, or resource specialists to see what programs are available for use in your classroom to assist readers at various stages of patterning practice or reading in general.

GRAY MATTER

For determining the success of strategies in the classroom, laboratory, computer, or interventions from reading specialists, tutors, or commercial reading programs, it would be most scientifically accurate to evaluate randomized, double-blind, placebo-controlled, multicenter studies that compare the brain activity of subjects who have received the specific intervention with those who have not. In addition, because there can be a positive effect on students just from spending time with an adult who appears interested in them (which is generally the experience of subjects in reading research protocols), there should be factoring in of that type of personal interaction for the control group. For example, the control group needs to spend equivalent time with the same group of evaluators as does the reading intervention group; however, this control group would work on a different task unrelated to reading. By keeping the variables as consistent as possible, there is greater likelihood that any difference in areas of brain activity that change in scans before and after the interventions will be measuring the intervention and not other factors that influenced the subjects' neural activity.

When well-controlled studies are conducted to evaluate strategy intervention success, by nonbiased researchers with no vested interest in or financing from the organizations who produce the intervention strategy, there can be valuable documentation of brain changes (or lack of changes) to then correlate with post-intervention cognitive testing of reading skills.

Currently, even in the studies of reading interventions that have been replicated and reported in peer-reviewed learning and language journals, the number of subjects is much smaller than the number of subjects in the studies I am used to reading in neurology journals when, for example, a new medication such as an anticonvulsant is being evaluated. One important aspect of medical trials is specificity of action. There are multiple types and causes of epilepsy and medical studies are expected to provide data about which type of epilepsy the new medication is best suited for. Similarly, there are many types of reading disorders.

As complex as the brain's reading networks appear to be, there are likely to be many places where reading success can be impacted. Vigilant educators and researchers will need to follow the research as to the long-term efficacy and response of large numbers of students from diverse backgrounds before educated matches of reading difficulties and reading

GRAY MATTER
(CONTINUED)

intervention can be made. Despite years of well controlled medical testing and follow-up in the treatment of epilepsy, my neurology colleagues and I have had to make our best deductions as to which anticonvulsant would be most effective for any given patient. There are so many individual variations and neural activities that remain uncertainties that judgment guides our medical decisions when some of the facts are still unknown. That is why during the treatment of many disorders—from epilepsy to ADHD—neurologists try one medication, and if it does not produce the desired result they switch to a second or even a third medication before beneficial results are achieved for the patient.

The "best medical judgment" model is essentially the state of reading intervention at this point. Just as there is no single pill for every person with epilepsy, there is no single reading program that will fit all students. To try to force one curriculum or reading intervention on all students with reading difficulties will surely leave more than one child behind.

Until there is a great deal more neurological, psychological, and cognitive research, the teaching of reading will continue to benefit from the use of a repertoire of strategies that powerfully engage the brain's reading systems. My understanding of the research leads me to conclude that three of the most critical components that teachers can bring to reading instruction are the promotion of pattern recognition, the consolidation of these patterns into stored memory, and the active engagement of students in mental manipulation of their newly patterned neural networks (through the higher cognitive processes of executive function). The teachers who make the greatest difference are likely to be those who weave their teaching art together with research-based reading strategies to give their students access to the gift of reading.

3

Fluency Building from the Brain to the Book

Fluency is the ability to read text accurately and quickly. Fluency means faster, smoother reading that approaches the speed of speech. When reading out loud, students with successful fluency read expressively, naturally, and effortlessly as they mentally divide the text into meaningful, distinct, related phrases. These students can decode accurately and rapidly, automatically group words appropriately, and scan ahead for cues such as punctuation. For students to know where to pause and when to change voice pitch, they need to decode while also scanning ahead to see how the sentence ends. The ability to read fluently allows students to understand and interact with what they read.

Fluency appears to be related to neural patterning from the visual sensory intake and print word processing areas in the occipital lobes. Neural networks connect the auditory processing centers in students' temporal lobes to their executive functioning and word identification centers in their prefrontal lobes (Geake, 2006). Fluent readers can decode, recognize, and comprehend the meaning of text at the same time, so their networks fire directly and efficiently. Reading practice reinforces the neural circuits that swiftly decode the written words, enabling students to look ahead and respond automatically to the punctuation at the end of a sentence, be it a question mark, exclamation point, or an adverb describing the state of the character—as in "he whispered anxiously."

Listening to and watching students read gives us insight into their fluency. Observe which students are automatically recognizing the words and punctuation as they read. Beginning readers focus their attention on deciphering individual words. Their oral reading may be incorrectly chunked and may sound flat and void of vocal inflection. Students who need to build fluency skills may make more frequent errors in both reading and comprehension because they are so focused on trying to read individual words that they are not able to successfully summarize or interpret what they have just read. Their brain networks may not be automatically processing recognized words and propelling this information to the executive function networks.

The visual input of the unfamiliar words may take a detour through decoding and pattern matching, which would disrupt fluency. With practice, as children increase their decoding skills and speed, they increase their neural processing efficiency and read with greater expression and comprehension.

GRAY MATTER

PET scans and fMRI scans suggest multiple reading networks in the brain working in parallel and in sequence to process, code, and retrieve the information that together results in reading fluency and comprehension. Before these networks were described, it was believed by many that reading was a left-brain activity (Jacobs, Schall, & Scheibel, 1993).

By 1998, neuroimaging evidence suggested that recognizing speech sounds, decoding written words, finding the meanings of words, comprehending complex text, making inferences, analyzing, and using the information from the reading to make new associations, appeared to stimulate neural subsystems in *both* brain hemispheres (Beeman & Chiarello, 1998). Of special significance to the reading processes of fluency beyond simple decoding is the brain's initial processing of new sensory input through short-term or working memory networks. It is this part of the memory system that appears to be critical to fluency development. This leads me to the strategies I suggest to allow the meaning of the decoded words to remain in memory long enough to connect with the other words in the sentence, paragraph, or page. The goal is for students to maintain the information in working memory long enough to make associations, recognize relationships, and pattern the information successfully into fluent reading.

Information from functional images and qEEG suggest connections between the brain's response to written text and metabolic activation in the alerting-association systems in the posterior left temporal and occipital lobes. It then appears that if the stimuli successfully pass through the affective filters and alerting systems, areas of stored related memories are activated to consolidate matching between the new data and information that has been previously stored (Coles, 2004).

PET scans show dramatic differences between a brain learning to *recognize* a category and one that has already *established* the category. This research supports a distinction between developing a skill and using it. Recognizing that particular information or sensory input fits into an established category correlates on scans with neural activation in the association-recognition systems. When the input is not recognized as having an association with previously stored data, the new information would need to be stored as a new recognition category (Peterson, Carpenter, & Fennema, 1988).

It follows that storing entirely new information would be less efficient and permanent than storing information that is linked to previous memories. Strategies to build category memory banks will be described in the comprehension chapter along with strategies aimed at increasing *relationships* between new and previously stored knowledge.

Once the recognition linkage is made, the new data (the word that was decoded) can remain in working memory long enough to have meaning. If the newly linked memory is then processed further through "mental manipulation" (cognitive processing in the prefrontal cortex), the information appears to have greater likelihood of becoming a stored long-term memory (Coles, 2004).

GRAY MATTER
(CONTINUED)

As more information is interpreted through neuroimaging about regional brain subspecialization, evidence is building to support the existence of such specialization in an executive function region of frontal lobes. There appear to be sections within the prefrontal cortex distinguishable on scans as especially active during judgment, analysis, prioritizing, organizing, direct- ing selective attentive focus, and sequencing. For example, the patterns and sequencing functions of concepts of print, turning pages, and reading print in the right direction are associated with neuroimaging activation within the executive function regions of the prefrontal cortex (McGaugh, McIntyre, & Power, 2002).

Verbal fluency is associated with increased metabolic activity in the left prefrontal cortex. Functional MRI scans localize activity in this same prefron- tal cortex region when executive function is engaged in by the subjects. The three tasks used that resulted in the activation of this proposed verbal fluency network were: having subjects repeat words they heard, say the opposite of the word, or say a word starting with a given letter (Phelps, Hyder, Blamire, & Shulman, 1997). Of interest is that the same executive function network activated during the executive function activities of analysis and judgment were also activated when subjects were shown patterns that stimulate the same eye movements that are made when readers move their eyes across a line of print as they read aloud with fluency (Pollatsek & Rayner, 1990). One interpretation is that the development of this part of the brain through activities that correlate with its neural activation on scans might increase a reader's potential to identify letters and words in the sequence of a sentence and turn them into meaning (Pollatsek & Rayner, 1990).

This chapter correlates the neurological research pertaining to building verbal or oral fluency with strategies based on my interpretations of this research and the ways it can be applied in the classroom. The fluency that is required for text comprehension will be covered in more detail in the comprehension chapter.

These and other brain research-based theories are the basis of the strategies I have applied with my students to build their fluency by constructing bridges between patterns of letters, word recognition, and comprehension. My interpretation of the research is that as the brain practices and builds neural networks that efficiently decode and recognize words, readers will not have to dedicate as much of their brain's processing activity to decoding, leaving more focus to attend to the meaning of text.

The goal of the strategies suggested here is to increase students' building of relational memories between the short-term memories that accompany newly read text and the information already stored in their background of knowledge.

Strategies to build decoding efficiency, word recognition speed, and fluency include model reading, rereading or choral reading, paired reading, independent reading, and tape-recorded reading. When students have multiple opportunities to read the same text with corrective feedback and enjoy the positive reinforcement of recognizing their progress, they are on the road to greater fluency.

Building Word Recognition Speed

Functional MRI scans done on average adult readers found a correlation between rapid automatized naming (RAN) activities (where they name items presented rapidly in a sequence) and increased neural activity in the same inferior frontal cortex brain regions activated when subjects engaged in more complex reading. Their success in the RAN tests also correlated with their complex reading skill (Misra, Katzir, Wolf, & Poldrack, 2004).

Most children and adults with fluency problems receive low scores on rapid naming. This correlation between the rapid naming area of brain activation and the inferior frontal cortex (one of the brain's most active reading and memory centers) is suggestive for strategies that build word recognition skills through practice in oral naming (Misra et al., 2004).

Although naming requires phonological processing, evidence suggests that naming speed is only modestly correlated with performance on phonological awareness tasks such as blending (Wagner, Torgesen, & Rashotte, 1994). The greatest correlation is between naming speed improvement and increased practice with letter and word identification tasks. In using this as a fluency-building strategy, students can practice naming familiar visual symbols (such as letters, numbers, or words) presented in random order (Wolf et al., 2002).

Rapid Naming Practice

I implemented rapid naming practice by having students create their own lists suited to their needs. After first using timed assessments of rapid naming of numbers, letters, or words (depending on my previous observations of the students' level of fluency), I determine what level of naming would be appropriate for them to work on. If their letter naming is slow, I have students make a stack of index cards with the letters printed on them. Other students make their stacks of cards with familiar words. Students' motivation increases because I offer lists of ability-appropriate words from which students can select the words for their practice. I have also created specific lists of words relating to topics of high interest to many students such as sports, music, and computers. The goal here is not for students to learn new words, but rather for students to increase the speed with which they can name familiar words. Practice sessions are scheduled during class, individually or in pairs (one student flips the cards while the partner responds), and for homework.

Some students don't concentrate well on this type of activity in the classroom, especially if they are easily distracted or have a hard time staying on task for repetition activities. Here, parent helpers are great resources when they can work with individual students in a quiet place outside the classroom. These practice sessions are not timed to keep stress down, but students know that they are working to increase their speed.

To further increase student motivation in this type of practice, I have students keep charts where they record their progress when we do periodic one-on-one timed measurement assessments of the number of words, letters, or numbers they read correctly in one minute. I show students how to graph their speed by counting the number of words, numbers, or letters read in a minute. Recognition of their progress appears to resonate with students' dopamine-pleasure response, affective filters, and goal-directed skills.

GRAY MATTER

Graphing is motivating because it makes progress evident. I help students set individually reachable but challenging WCPM (words correct per minute) goals. Practice in word or symbol naming with visible, charted progress toward their desired goal promotes their perseverance, just as seeing improvement in running speed motivates track activity participants or charting weight loss motivates dieters. The ability to see that their rereading efforts pay off over time allows students to tolerate occasional failures as they pursue fluency. For less fluent readers, monitoring their individual progress is especially valuable when they have felt frustrated by previous comparisons to classmates. They experience a sense of accomplishment when they recognize that their effort resulted in progress.

These charts can be even more helpful if students and teachers work together to build student metacognition strategies. Students can be prompted to think about what they did that resulted in the improvements on their charts. If they write down their strategy, such as "More practice with the taped reading" or "More reading with my partner," they will learn which strategies are best for their learning styles and expand the use of these strategies into other reading and learning situations.

Although it is not always engaging to review and rehearse word lists with flash cards, this type of activity can be made more engaging when students have input, such as selecting which cards they want to work on—words about the ocean or words about outer space. Students also can make their index cards from approved lists of words with high interest to them that are still in their independent reading range. Then the focus is on building speed because accuracy is already there.

The object is not for students to memorize new sight words, but rather to promote neural activity in their inferior frontal lobes as they respond to items presented rapidly in a sequence. The hope is that stimulation of the neuronal circuits in this important reading network will carry over into reading fluency.

Repeated Reading

Repeated reading is a strategy that can be used when students in a class are at different levels of fluency. It works best when done in small groups based on fluency level. Word-by-word readers or those who have difficulty sounding out words need more instruction and practice in fluent application of phonics to single words and practice recognizing high frequency words so they can read orally at their decodable instructional level.

More advanced fluency students can work to build fluency with more complex words and at their higher instructional level. Even very skilled readers may read in a slow, deliberate manner when reading texts with many unfamiliar words or topics. The goal of fluency building, ability-level rereading is to provide individualized opportunities for skill growth. This means reading groups need to be small enough to be low stress and to offer each student enough time to orally reread several times, with guidance, so fluency can truly improve. When small groups are beyond your resources as an individual classroom teacher, instructional aides, parent helpers, peer partners, response reading with audiotapes, and computer assisted oral reading can help.

The practice of repeated reading builds fluency in a way similar to the RAN practice, but by using student-level decodable text instead of individual cards. Students repeatedly read the same text until the words are so familiar that they can attend to more than sounding out individual words and look ahead at the sentence to use word and punctuation cues to add expression to their voice and comprehension to their reading. Repeated reading, especially of predictable, patterned stories, is consistent with my interpretation of teaching in a manner structured to be brain compatible.

The best text material to use in oral rereading is material that is interesting to students. Text material should also be appropriately challenging (just above their independent reading level). I select decodable books that are high interest, based my students' interests, current activities in their lives, or their response to other topics we are investigating in cross-curricular activities. I alternate between repeated reading books I select and those that students in each fluency ability group choose from those I preselect based on the group's instructional level. I look for decodables that are not predictable in rhyme or repetition style because the goal is not memorization of a script, but increasing familiarity with the actual reading of each word. After I read the text aloud, I start the rereading process with a passage of 50-100 words.

To decrease stress, lower affective filters, and make the very first exposure to the book more pleasurable, students can have the option of simply listening without trying to follow along in their decodables or with a big book. For the second reading, students follow along and I let them know when to turn the page so they'll be able to keep up even if they haven't followed the text.

Guided Rereading

To assure unobstructed passage of the visual text input to the hippocampus, the text for rereading practice needs to be within a comfort zone of independent reading success so the focus will not be on decoding, but on the development of fluency.

After my initial read-aloud, the whole group rereads the passage with me. For each subsequent reading, I emphasize just one of the punctuation marks or other cues, such as pauses for commas or raising of pitch when sentences end with question marks. I guide and model reading connected phrases and clauses without breaks.

When individuals want to try reading the passage independently they can volunteer to do so. When most students can successfully reread several passages without my help (I gradually lower the volume of my speech and walk around the group as they read to hear individuals), I divide the students into pairs or threesomes and they reread several passages to one another. When the pairs are ready, I listen to them read. For homework, students are encouraged to read their passages to family members.

After successful rereading activities in class, I explain the strategy of rereading as it can apply to independent reading. I ask student volunteers to model the strategy with a new passage or book. I explain that when they are reading independently and come to a word that is unfamiliar and not immediately decodable, they should ask for help and then read and reread the sentence aloud as they gain fluency.

The time when students have begun to decode with increasing fluency is a critical period to motivate them as readers. Engaging books are not always part of packaged reading curriculum that is phonics-heavy. As you go through decodable books seeking ones for fluency practice, look for books at students' reading levels that offer opportunities for them to practice sound-letter correspondence and decoding, that are engaging, and that include and emphasize the newly learned pairings. The motivation needed for students to want to reread these decodable texts is critical if the pairings they learn are to be reinforced and add to their fluency.

Word recognition and decoding appear most brain compatible when the practice activities are about personally relevant topics. As will be described in the chapter on destressing reading, without the positive motivation, engagement, and personal connections some decodable texts can be alienating. Effective stress reducing and positively motivating strategies are needed to facilitate the processing of decoding patterns so the decoded word can pass unhindered through the affective filters to enter brain patterning and be expressed in fluent reading. If word recognition is not learned successfully, students will be stuck in unfulfilling, slow, and laborious reading.

Modeling Fluency

Begin any modeling activity, such as the one that precedes a rereading lesson, by describing the goals of the activity to build student connection and focus. If your students are all at the same level of English literacy and won't be confused by modeling the correct and incorrect fluency, it helps to emphasize the things you are listening for by exaggerating fluent and non-fluent reading. The caution here is to be sure that the incorrect modeling is not similar to the errors frequently made by specific students. If that is the case, I stick to modeling the proper fluency.

When modeling, I use humor and exaggeration to keep students interested, and we discuss cartoon characters that are known for very artificially deliberate speech errors or overly slurred, mumbled, barely understandable speech. (Again, this is not done when a student in the class has a similar speech problem.) When students ask about stutterers or other people with speech disorders who are not fluent speakers, we use the teachable moment to revisit the topic of responding to people with differences. Because our supportive classroom community is built from the first day with an emphasis on respect (for oneself, others, and our planet) the stage is set for these types of discussions.

Modeling Supportive Reading

Supportive reading groups require that students are comfortable with the activity, without embarrassment or boredom, and with enough intrinsic reinforcement to motivate them to persevere. The setting must be low stress. Small groups should have opportunities to work together supportively and to practice the appropriate responses to classmates' errors and successes. Preparatory modeling of these appropriate responses can begin in a nonreading activity response to open-ended, student centered questions such as, "What did you do this weekend?" to give students the experience of speaking to the class and listening attentively with proper response behavior. When students have developed the ability to listen respectfully, without snickering or correcting their classmates, they are ready for small group rereading activities. When appropriate, it does help to model the difference between smooth, fluent, expressive reading and choppy, incorrectly punctuated reading. I demonstrate using my voice at higher and lower pitches, volumes, and speeds, and we discuss how it changes the meaning of the words. Students then take turns selecting the way they want the sentence to sound (angry, frightened, assertive, secretive). Volunteers read the sentence their "way" and call on classmates to guess what their intent was. I had originally done this by having the volunteer first whisper to a partner or to me what his or her intent was, but when there were errors in interpretation or even in the demonstration some students were frustrated. By not having the readers reveal intent first, the students have the option of accepting any reasonable interpretation made by a classmate. This does not reduce the effectiveness of the lesson because students are still practicing the finer aspects of expressive fluency following my modeling.

Choral Reading

Choral reading gives students the experience of reading aloud without the stress of reading alone. Based upon the previously described research demonstrating that repeated stimulation of neuronal networks increases their efficiency, it makes sense that the experience of reading aloud together reinforces patterns.

When we start the choral reading, I ask students to whisper the words as I read aloud. This process continues until students become more confident. As the reading progresses and I drop my volume, students begin to read more loudly. At first it may be the louder readers who can give confidence to the others to follow as long as I intervene to keep a reasonable pace. Eventually, as the vocabulary of the new book becomes more familiar and content and prediction kick in to increase fluency, I drop my voice down in volume and distinctly mouth the words.

Individualized and Paired Activities

After students have built confidence, lowered stress, and opened flow through their affective filters, they are ready for more individualized guidance through a variety of activities to build fluency.

Student-Adult Reading

In student-adult reading, students read one-on-one at their fluency level with a parent, classroom aide, or teacher. As in choral reading, first the adult models, then individual students whisper-repeat along with the adult, and then alone. The adult can scaffold the student's reading by joining in for corrective feedback until, with the lowered affective filter, the practice gradually builds student speed, accuracy, and expressiveness in oral reading. This adult modeling may be providing the mirror neuron stimulation for students to use to pattern their own reading.

Partner Reading

Partner reading pairs more fluent readers with less fluent readers as they take turns reading aloud to each other. This activity requires modeling and explicit instruction in proper behavior and in what comments or corrections are appropriate. Students are motivated to follow these rules because they want the privilege of working with partners.

I have found that this activity is most successful at building student confidence and skill when prearranged modeling by a rehearsed pair of students precedes it. Students see how partners acknowledge each other even for trying. "That was a great first try." (That encouragement from a partner is the type of intrinsic reward that increases dopamine release and the positive benefits of this neurotransmitter.) The pair that models the activity can be coached to make corrective comments in appropriate language that includes something positive with each correction, such as, "Your reading speed and volume were very good. Now you can change your voice to show that this sentence is a question."

For this activity, use short, interesting texts at the level of the less fluent reader and prepare the pair with prereading teacher modeling. Use texts with content that relates to the students' lives and, ideally, texts that relate to shared class experiences. Other text choices are books with information that the class has heard or read about previously. First, the more fluent reader reads a sentence or paragraph. (The amount of reading done before the second student repeats the reading needs to be predetermined and kept short enough to keep both readers engaged.) Then the less fluent reader reads the same text. While the second reader reads, the first reader needs to let the less fluent reader try to work out challenging words or phrases before giving hints to model the correct reading. Both readers use the supportive words of encouragement they have practiced and seen modeled by student-reader pairs who demonstrated the activity before students work in their independent pairs.

If the more fluent reader gives corrective help, the rules are that the second reader rereads the sentence or passage until he or she reads it independently with expressiveness and accuracy. (Strategy adapted from Meyer & Felton, 1999.) Designations can be made in the text as to where the pair should stop, summarize, personalize, and connect. For example, I use the code *SSPC* and write it in appropriate places in the text. Students then take turns following the code.

Stop: The student reading the passage says, "I'll stop now for SSPC."

Summarize: The student who read the passage summarizes the content. The other member of the pair can add information.

Personalize: The student who read the passage relates the material to a personal experience or describes how he or she might someday be in a similar situation. The partner does the same.

Connect: The student who read the passage connects the material to something previously read or seen in a film, preferably one that was a shared class experience for both students in the pair. The partner does the same or adds more detail.

These prompts may stimulate relational memories that become available as memory templates for the text being read. Just as fluent reading builds comprehension, comprehension increases when text is connected with stored memories and prior knowledge. The increased comprehension then adds success to the subsequent oral reading, which becomes more accurate and fluent.

Tape-Assisted Reading

Tape-assisted reading allows students to read and reread books along with a recording they select from a shelf or box designated by independent reading levels. Students who feel uncomfortable reading in front of another person benefit a great deal from this activity.

For the first listening, the student listens to the tape and points to the words as he or she hears them read. In subsequent listenings, students read the words they can along with the tape. An assessment takes place when the students decide they are ready to read the book aloud to you without the tape. Students can bring the books home to read to their families as a reward for successful mastery of the fluent, expressive reading of the book.

When I make these tapes I follow the format of the premade ones and use a bell or other sound to alert the reader to turn the page. You can create tapes for a variety of fluency levels and to emphasize different aspects of fluency. In some tapes you can emphasize phrasing and have two types of read-along books available—one with slash marks between chunks and one without the marks. Computer-assisted recording such as that available with Macintosh *GarageBand* software allows you to add variable speed for rereading practice. My students have used the computer technology to make their own read-aloud original books (very inspiring for reluctant writers who enjoy computer technology) for classmates to share or to give to younger siblings. I don't want to distract the students' concentration on fluency so I don't add music to my tapes, but I do allow the adding of sound effects and music to student-produced recorded book projects.

Strategies to Build Fluency Through Intelligence Strengths

Howard Gardner developed the theory that intelligence is made up of distinct learning proficiencies that can work individually or together. In 1983, Gardner reported seven such learning strengths or styles, which he called intelligences. In 1996 he added an eighth, naturalist intelligence (Gardner, 1999). Using multiple intelligences as a guide allows you to vary fluency activities to engage students' dominant intelligences. I have interpreted these intelligences by considering which fluency-promoting activities might best fit with the proposed brain response networks associated with their learning strengths. This is another area where I am making the connections based on my understanding and interpretation of the brain-learning research. However, controlled research studies with neuroimaging and cognitive testing have not been done on these strategies.

Linguistic intelligence is characterized by sensitivity to the meaning and order of words. Students with linguistic intelligence are adept at using language to understand and convey information. They are often sensitive to the nuances, order, and rhythm of words. Students I have worked with who have strengths in linguistic intelligence enjoy reading activities that include rhymes, verbal word games, telling stories, reading silently, and reading aloud. With strengths in vocabulary building, memorizing, and learning foreign languages, these students appear to have greater development in auditory processing that facilitates their auditory learning skills. These students are more likely to recall what they hear, follow spoken instructions, and build fluency by listening and speaking. They are often the leading voices that build group confidence and skills in choral reading and repeated reading. These verbal learners can also be excellent partners in paired oral reading.

Musical-rhythmic intelligence can include sensitivity to pitch and rhythm of sounds and responsiveness to listening to or performing music. These students might be able to hear a song or tune and remember, play, or sing its melody without printed music. With students with musical-rhythmic intelligence, I use fluency strategies where learning is connected to rhythmic constructs. These students have been particularly responsive to the placement of strategic slash marks as cues that chunk words correctly for fluent reading. These students are also engaged by choral reading.

Logical-mathematical intelligence is reflected in understanding abstractions, cause-and-effect, and code and pattern recognition. These analytic learners respond to fluency activities presented in sequential steps, with rules and examples, teacher-directed lessons, clear goals and requirements. Children with strong logical-mathematical intelligence often prefer to make decisions based on logic and respond to knowing the reasons behind our rules of punctuation. Because they tend to focus on details and facts, they seem to enjoy the opportunity to preview text independently before the class activity, often after teacher modeling. This may help them analyze the punctuation and use the rules they have learned to determine where natural pauses or voice inflections are appropriate. These learners also enjoy creating and even designing their own goal-assessment charts and graphs to follow their progress. If properly coached in cooperative community behavior, these students can help classmates create and add data to their own assessment graphing charts.

Visual-spatial intelligence is related to aptitude in understanding the relationships of objects, concepts, or images in different fields or dimensions. Visual learners may have more developed occipital lobe visual processing and relational memory connections to objects and words they see. They are especially responsive to lessons where I incorporate visual observations of the punctuation and text as they watch a fluent reader model the facial and lingual movements of the associated oral reading. These students seem to benefit a great deal from independent practice, such as with note cards and RAN activities, to build their fluency speed.

Bodily-kinesthetic intelligence includes the ability to use fine and gross motor skills in visual or performing arts, physical play, sports, and object manipulative activities. My more tactile students respond well to word or letter cards as prompts for oral fluency practice just as they enjoy using sandpaper letters when learning to recognize letters and make sound associations. Because they appear to recall what they touch, their fluency seems to respond to actually feeling the movement in their lips and faces when they read with expression.

The more kinesthetic students in this category are excited about activities where they trace or draw letters in sand, water, or in the air. To build fluency, they enjoy adding movements to their verbal expressiveness such as in Readers' Theater activities where they use their body awareness to move their bodies to connect with text and convey expressiveness. When doing oral reading with tapes, they add verbal fluency by occasionally working with hand puppets or watching their faces in mirrors to react kinesthetically to text.

Interpersonal intelligence is evident in children who work well with others and in group learning activities. They tend to be perceptive and responsive to others' moods and feelings. Their ability to interact with others with understanding and to interpret classmates' behaviors makes these students well suited for peer/paired reading leadership roles, such as peer models before the class tries new fluency activities, and they are helpful verbal prompters in choral reading. They seem to particularly enjoy choosing books about interpersonal relationships.

Intrapersonal intelligence can be apparent in students with dedication to and understanding of their own beliefs and goals. They are more independent and less likely to be influenced by what others think of them. These students seem to form their most successful relational memories when they are able to link the text to their personal experiences or to positive emotional connections. They enjoy working independently at goals they help establish and they enjoy tape-supported or one-on-one work with adults, rather than with peers, for fluency practice. They sometimes need to be permitted to whisper even after the first repeated oral reading in group situations. These students also tend to respond well to the graphing of their self-timed fluency assessments and making meta-cognition notes in writing instead of verbalizing them.

Technology for Fluency

Computerized reading fluency programs have been used to assess individual student fluency and adjust instruction to suit the needs of each reader. Neuroimaging is becoming more helpful in determining which students are most likely to benefit from computerized interventions. I have found computer technology helpful using visual and auditory input that highlights patterns for fluency practice. Students build speed and accuracy through practice with the patterns of oral expression for phrase chunking, punctuation response, and content influence on verbal expressiveness. Even basic word processing programs can be used to highlight what is being emphasized through changes in color, size, font, animation, or grouping.

When considering the currently available and future computer programs to improve student fluency, look for programs with flexible responsiveness, a variety of activities for motivating fluency-building practice for students with different learning style preferences, and programs that incorporate simultaneous assessment, guidance, and opportunities for students to choose materials. Specific guidance for fluency-building software may be available from school districts' reading, curriculum, or technology specialists.

GRAY MATTER

A collaborative study from neurocognitive researchers at Cornell University and University of Pennsylvania studied reading levels of children ages 6 to 9 with behavioral and fMRI scans before and after two types of interventions. The children were assigned to their groups randomly, not based on their reading differences. One group participated in The Reading Works (TRW), a computerized program of word building focusing on letter-sound relationships within visual-word forms. The other program, Guided Reading (GR), uses authentic texts to guide reading programs based on feedback from periodic comprehension assessments built into the programs. Each group of students received twenty 40-minute sessions of one-on-one tutoring with their program.

The researchers interpreted their data to suggest that the type of intervention influenced different reading skills and appeared to be associated with increased brain activity in the predicted regions of the brain most associated on scans with decoding activities. The type of educational environment was found to modulate the degree to which the initial activity predicted reading behavioral outcomes. The amount of measured improvement in students receiving TRW correlated with increased activity in the upper temporal lobe brain areas that had been found to be most active during phonological processing and decoding. Similarly, the amount of cognitively measured improvement in students receiving the GR intervention correlated with increased activity in the frontal lobe brain and lower left temporal areas that have been associated with whole word recognition (Ochs et al., 2005).

One implication of these preliminary studies is that if and when cognitive science working with neuroimaging studies confirms the differentiation of brain regions as clearly linked to subtypes of fluency, such as in phonological processing, decoding, or recognizing whole words, that information might help match the type of intervention with an individual student's needs. If the results are confirmed in follow-up cognitive and fMRI pre- and post-intervention studies and the correlations continue to be consistent, the hope is that the fMRI images would not be necessary if the reading skill cognitive tests can adequately predict both fMRI findings and the type of intervention that is best suited for the child.

There are a great deal of "ifs" here, but as more data comes in providing strong correlations between cognitive testing, fMRI studies, and student response to specific fluency interventions, computer assisted instruction could play a big part in implementing individually constructed intervention, assessment, and feedback programs. In the meantime, let us be wary of the business that reading intervention has become. For example, most of the available training programs require a great commitment of time and money, with a standard training protocol (100 minutes a day, five days a week) representing more than one-third of students' school instruction time (*Nature Neuroscience,* 2004).

4

Eliminating Barriers on the Road to Fluency

Students who struggle with fluency are aware that they don't read aloud with the expressiveness and correct pronunciation used by their classmates. They know that they take much longer to read the same amount of text and that they don't comprehend the text as well as their classmates. This stress can further decrease students' successful patterning and processing of what they read. They can become more anxious about reading aloud and, as a result, make more errors or take fewer potential risks by not reading with expression.

To permit information to travel effectively through the limbic system to be processed and stored as word memories or decoding skills, it is necessary to create a classroom environment that is supportive and makes students feel safe. In a classroom where diversity is honored and mistakes are recognized as opportunities to learn, students develop the trust that is critical if they are to persevere and take the risk of reading aloud to build fluency. Students need to know that classmates will not laugh at their mistakes and that teachers will judge them on effort and progress, not just on outcome.

For students who need more self-confidence, it helps to have activities that allow them to recognize their own improvement and to measure their success toward their own goals. A supportive class environment built from the start is one where classmates also acknowledge their peers' progress rather than product. Students who see their own charted progress on individual WPM graphs and who hear acknowledgment from classmates and the teacher for their improvement begin to approach oral reading with more confidence and a more positive, optimistic attitude. They appear to develop higher frustration tolerance as they see their read-aloud errors as part of the learning process and not as shameful embarrassments.

Students who lack confidence in their oral reading fluency are likely to refuse to read aloud to a group, but some may be willing to practice with supportive peer partners or other adults such as aides and parent classroom helpers. The first task is to help these reluctant students overcome the habits they may have acquired such as making self-derogatory statements, becoming easily frustrated and defensive, and being vulnerable to perceived peer judgment.

When students feel threatened, anxious, embarrassed, or intimidated, especially in situations involving reading, their emotional blockage in the amygdala interferes with the cognition needed to select out the important information (Ornstein & Sobel, 1987). Because emotional comfort is so important to reading, brain-friendly destressing strategies and building a classroom community of nonjudgmental, cooperative learners will support struggling readers and enable them to grow in their zones of comfort and proximal development to advance in literacy.

Student-Centered Discussion

As students become more familiar with the vocabulary of the book, especially new words and specialty words that have been previewed and reviewed in vocabulary practice, they can build their fluency with these words if student-centered discussions are framed to include the new words. Student-centered discussions are open-ended so there are no right or wrong answers.

Prepare students by having volunteers review the content of the story. Select discussion topics inspired by the story, especially aspects of the book that students can connect with their own lives and experiences to engage their attention and motivation to participate. Look at the KWL for "Want to know questions" that students suggested themselves.

Before some discussions, give students time to look through class, school library, or the Internet for information that pertains to the story and connects with their interests. This will give reluctant readers and speakers more pleasure and confidence as they join in the discussion by offering information they "own" because they found it.

The scaffolding for the discussion is to write the important vocabulary words on the board or chart and when possible, students also refer to their notes from the vocabulary preview. With each response to a discussion question, the students are requested to include one of the vocabulary words in their comment.

Example: When we read *Black Star, Bright Dawn* by Scott O'Dell, I listed the words we had previewed, such as musher, landscape, horizon, arctic, and others, and selected questions from the students' "Want to know" list that I believed had general appeal and would provide opportunities to use the vocabulary words. Interest-related questions have included:

• What makes conditions harsh on the Iditarod trail?

• How is your dog like and different from Bright Dawn's sled dogs?

• If you were a musher, what would you be alert for along the trail?

To make the class discussion more novel I had prepared a "snowball" by putting crushed ice in foil in the shape of a circle and freezing it with added water so it stayed round. I then covered it with white paper and brought it to school in another bag of ice to keep it cold.

When students wanted to participate in the discussion they would raise their hands, then the last student who had responded and still held the snowball would gently (as we modeled and practiced) toss it to them. Other times I've used koosh balls for this, had the vocabulary themed discussions in a circle around a lit candle, or had the speaker wear a hat related to the book's theme. These extra props increase student engagement and may add a flashbulb memory to the vocabulary word and comprehension review while increasing the dopamine-pleasure response.

Lesson Considerations: Some students will gain confidence in using the vocabulary words in their discussion comments if they practice first with supportive peers.

Thematic Units

The most important question a student in my class should be able to answer at any time, during any lesson, is "Why is this important enough for me to learn it?" My years as a clinical neurologist and research neuroscientist, as well as the current brain imaging scans taken while subjects actually learn new material, continue to support the notion that the person who thinks, learns. That is, truly learns, in the sense that the new information is successfully stored in the brain's long-term neuronal circuitry so it can be accessed and retrieved when needed.

One of the best ways I have found for adding incentive for students to build fluency is by incorporating fluency-building activities into cross-curricular themes that are meaningful to each child and integrate with the curriculum.

Sample Thematic Lessons That Incorporate Fluency-Building Activities

Ethics

In my cross-curricular unit on ethics and ethical dilemmas, I use the *big-picture-first* approach by starting with guest speakers on a

wide variety of real world situations where the people struggle with
ethical dilemmas: law, religion, medicine, business. For students
who need fluency-building confidence I see if any of their family
members or family friends can be included as these class speakers. When suitable, I encourage and help the student prepare to
introduce the speaker he or she knows using vocabulary we have
previewed about ethics and ethical dilemmas.

Challenge and Exploration

I have used the cross-curricular theme of "Challenge and Exploration" at the start of the school year so students are in a comfort
zone and have shared experiences such as the challenge of a new
teacher, classroom, books, more homework, new classmates, or
other common challenges. Parent and community speakers add to
the students' appreciation of the relevance of what they study and
again help fluency-challenged students feel more a part of the unit
and community if they know the speaker or the organization or if
they help me with the planning. During the Challenge and Exploration theme, we have had speakers with expertise in Columbus,
the importance of sugar in the history of the developing world,
the earliest maps used by the explorers of the New World, the lives
of the poor seamen, the value of historical novels, and early navigational science as well as a variety of speakers who describe their
own experiences either overcoming challenges or related to exploration. For homework, students explore their heritage. Some students
can, through parental or grandparent interviews, trace back their
heritage to family members who immigrated to the United States
seeking improvement or more opportunities in religious, financial,
social, or political aspects of their lives. Parents who were immigrants themselves can share their experiences with the class. Pairs
of students "explore" each other's past heritage, in keeping with
discovering similarities with why the colonists and subsequent
immigrants came to the New World in search of a better life and
how those early settlers were similar or different from their own

family members with respect to challenges faced. Class discussion follows the pair-share. Student pairs next share feelings about the challenges they expect in the coming school year. Their partner then introduces them to the class using the information gleaned during a series of guided, information gathering interviews.

Lesson Consideration: I provide interest inventory sheets for students to fill out and use as prompts for asking questions and recalling their answers during the peer interviews. The students who need extra time or support can work on these at home with parents or in class with adult assistance.

Student pairs have lists of the vocabulary words we are learning that are new and important to our reading in literature and history. Pairs practice responding with encouragement when a partner uses one of the words as well as making a check next to the word on their list. I circulate and ask students to use one of the words I see checked on their list by speaking it in a sentence to me. If they make pronunciation errors I repeat their sentence with the correct pronunciation and use the word again as I emphasize the accurate parts of their sentences. By not directly saying, "You are incorrect, here is the right way to do it" I am still giving corrective feedback while supporting student effort through incorporating what they "got right" into the amended sentence.

Paired work is followed by whole-class discussions where students have their lists as scaffolding and share their pair-developed ideas about the challenges of the new school year. They are required to include one of the vocabulary words they have practiced. To build fluency, students have time to first write their comments down. They read from their own words after practicing these with their partner to build fluency before reading to the class. The goal is to build reading fluency by having students incorporate vocabulary words into self and pair-constructed sentences they first practice, then read aloud. Because these have personal and thematic relevance, they are more likely to feel positive about the activity. Practicing with a peer builds confidence and fluency.

Lesson Consideration: When students are fluency-challenged, I listen to them practice with their peers and give supportive, corrective feedback until they are able to read their comments fluently without embarrassment.

We read a class literature book about challenge that coincides with our historical study of the explorers of the New World and their challenges, such as an easier reading modified version of *Two Years Before the Mast*. To prepare for student oral reading they practice reading sections to partners. Students needing fluency support are given preselected sections that they will be reading aloud. They have opportunities to practice rereading their sections at home and with partners. Instead of reading in a circle where it would be obvious when I call on a student to read out of order, I call on students to read sections. Most students are selected randomly, but when I come to the specially marked sections of my book with the student's name noted, I call on that pre-rehearsed student to read his or her section.

With some classes I include a discussion about the challenges of reading aloud and ask volunteers to give their answers to the question, "The sailors on the ship from our book, *The Pilgrim*, faced many challenges we have been reading about. Sometimes, just reading aloud in class is a challenge. Who would like to share why it might be challenging for you to read aloud?" To show students that they are not isolated in their reading anxiety, I encourage classmates to raise hands if they share the same fear just stated by the volunteer.

Independent reading for book report choices is guided for independent skill level. Choice is again a positive motivating factor and I provide a variety of books pertaining to our theme. I ask students to include oral reading from their books as part of their book reports. The students who need more goal-specific fluency guidance meet with me and show me several choices they have made to read aloud. I guide them to select the passage with achievable challenge and that is the one they practice at home or with class partners.

Lesson Consideration: I often meet with the students who need the advantages of choice to reduce the negative responses they have developed to oral reading. At these meetings they have first choice of available topics. Sometimes we visit the school library together after I have consulted with our librarian who helps preselect appropriate books for the student's reading level and interests.

Engaging the cooperative and collaborative skills through recreation of the historical events they read about in literature and history texts is another useful way to promote fluent reading practice. This is similar to reader's theater, but because of the students' personal connection to the cross-curricular unit of challenge and exploration, the skits are especially significant to them. Students work in groups I prearrange for complementary interests, skills, and fluency to strengthen social and reading support. The goal is for students to practice reading aloud words with connection to text that will build their fluency while their affective filters are not stressed.

I give each group a portion of the text to portray in their skit (e.g., pages 6-14 or the subchapter on the Rhode Island settlement). I give a list of specific points and vocabulary from the section that I want them to include in their skits and an associated passage of text to be read aloud. There is one of these specific points per student. When the students choose the one they will focus on, they have the positive brain benefits of choice that are detailed in a later chapter, including the enhanced dopamine release.

Lesson Consideration: Through modeling and practice the students have learned and become comfortable with a style of teaching that follows the philosophy that each student has equal opportunities for success at their best level. Students understand that this means that not all student assignments are the same. For the choice system to work you may need to let the lower-fluency students have an early choice and be sure that the passages available include ones they will like and feel comfortable reading. Even in lower elementary grades I have found that when I start the year explaining my philosophy of equal not always meaning the same for every student, I encourage students to conference with me when they think they would benefit from accommodations to suit their ability levels, unique talents, or interests.

The group creates the rest of their script, either with formal writing or repeated improvisational practice. Each time they rehearse, they each read their special segment as part of their "lines." They use the modeled practice procedures for readers' theater, whereby they give each other positive feedback and then corrective feedback about how to improve inflection or pronunciation to be more "dramatic." The scaffolding of skit presentation makes it less embarrassing to read with expression because students have seen and we have discussed the difference between dramatic speech in plays and everyday conversational speech.

Audience response to the skit is encouraged after the class is reminded that only positive comments are appropriate in this postproduction period because corrections and advice were offered during skit preparation and now is the time to celebrate success.

Just as audience response celebrates successful aspects of the skit presentations, I incorporate celebrations as culminating activities in cross-curricular thematic units. This is not specifically a reading event, but I do incorporate oral reading when possible. For example, after this theme of challenge and exploration we celebrate with a few hours in a local park doing exploration such as a guided walk with a naturalist who shows us which plants and trees could have been used by early settlers in this region for food, clothes, or building supplies. We often eat food, prepared by student-parent volunteers, that has historical-regional relevance and is made from ingredients available to the earliest native residents or settlers. I have included a "campfire" sometimes in a BBQ pit or simply around a large candle when students read a passage from any of their books or personal writing journals that are meaningful to them. Again, the selected reading is one that I guide specific students to practice before the celebration day.

Technology for Stress-Free Fluency Practice

I've found that children enjoy writing on white boards, even more than blackboards. Technology can engage students with programs such as using electronic whiteboards connected to computers where they can use special markers or even their fingers to perform activities to build decoding and fluency at their own pace. Exercises are available such as circling the "naming" and "describing" words in sentences or highlighting letter combinations at the beginning and end of words. There is the added benefit of tactile involvement to stimulate multisensory memory networks.

Benefits of computer adjuncts to fluency practice include:

• Appropriate challenge. Good computer fluency building programs use assessments and feedback to find the students' ZPD (zone of proximal development) and adjust the challenge levels for individual students. This responsive lesson adaptation can provide exactly the right level of challenge with the appropriate scaffolding to bridge students to the next level of skill. For students of different skill levels the privacy of computer work minimizes the concern about social embarrassment they may feel about incorrect verbal responses in class.

• Practice without teachers. After direct instruction and classroom activities, computer practice can give students immediate feedback, correction, practice, and reinforcement with fluency building programs at their instructional level when you are working with other students.

• Incremental challenge. The best fluency programs work in a similar manner as computer or video games, offering incremental levels of challenge and accommodating students' varied strengths and limitations of their sensory, motor, cognitive, motivational, and affective systems.

• Experience the program. In selecting computer programs for fluency practice, it is advisable to try the systems yourself. Important considerations are the clarity of the visual display and auditory outputs. If the students need to tape record and then listen to their reading, it helps to have variable speed control to slow down playback rate without distorting their recorded voices, especially when they are working on expressiveness. Most systems have Web site demonstrations available or your district resource specialists may know of other schools with systems you can try out.

• Some programs offer speech synthesizers or screen readers that display and read aloud (or through headphones) the text on a computer screen as students follow along verbally. If expressiveness and response to punctuation are goals, the computerized "speech" should sound realistic and appropriate.

• Adaptations are also available that respond and adjust for varied backgrounds in exposure to literacy, language, culture, and learning style preferences. For example, the *Wiggleworks* program includes a read-aloud section where children can listen to books read by children with different regional accents. Adaptations and choices that have positive impact on students' affective states can be useful resources for increasing students' response to and participation in the computer program.

• In addition to fluency building, programs are available to build comprehension and response to reading activities using computer generated, ability-suited prompts such as leading questions, suggested strategies, and graphic organizer formats. These programs can add assessment potential when students can demonstrate comprehension through *input* of their recorded reading or verbal responses to computer generated image prompts relative to the text they have just read. These are recorded so the students can listen to their own responses and rerecord if they want to improve. Then you can listen at any time to their recordings for assessment purposes.

You have probably recognized many similarities between the activities I use to destress fluency practice and those you use to build student reading skills. That is good news, because now the neuroimaging research is providing support for these strategies and your continued use of them. Highly structured reading curriculum programs can consume many classroom hours. Still, with your understanding of how the brain builds fluency best when lessons are R.A.D. (*reticular activating system* out of stress/threat mode, *affective amygdala filter* primed to admit knowledge to cognitive centers, and *dopamine* release in response to pleasure) you can select strategies to help students' brains work at high efficiency to build stress free fluency.

5

Vocabulary Building and Keeping

Rich vocabulary reflects success in almost every region of the brain, from rote memory through working and relational memory, categorizing, connecting, patterning, storage, and executive function. Functional MRI and PET scans of the individual processes that go into word learning and usage suggest that, like reading, vocabulary processing requires students to organize their thoughts through neural networks connecting brain regions in several lobes.

If you have studied a foreign language, you may recall how basic your early sentences were and how limited they were in texture and depth. With enhanced vocabulary, students grow in skills of verbal fluency, writing, and comprehension. The National Reading Panel states that the larger the students' vocabulary, the more adept they are at understanding text (National Reading Panel, 2000). When students build vocabulary mastery, they can more effectively communicate their ideas, knowledge, and voice.

The Vocabulary Gap

Vocabulary knowledge in young children directly affects their later success in learning to read (Roit, 2002). Children who enter school with limited vocabulary knowledge fall even further behind over time in reading fluency and comprehension (Baker, Simmons, & Kame'enui, 1997).

Orally tested vocabulary at the end of 1st grade is considered
a significant predictor of reading comprehension 10 years later
(Cunningham & Stanovich, 1997). If vocabulary is not enriched
by 3rd grade, children have declining comprehension scores in the
later elementary years (Chall, Jacobs, & Baldwin, 1990). If there
is no intervention, vocabulary-deficient students will not reach the
estimated 15,000 root words known by the average 12th grade
student (Biemiller, 2001).

These concerns indicate that steps need to be taken to narrow
the gap as soon as children begin kindergarten with the goal of
reaching a speaking and listening vocabulary of between 2,500 and
5000 words by the end of kindergarten (McKeown & Beck, 1988).
If this early vocabulary intervention is accomplished and sustained
so that students increase their vocabulary by between 3,000 and
4,000 words per year, they should reach appropriate vocabulary,
as measured by what an individual can use and understand when
writing or reading, as they continue through elementary school
(Anderson, 1999; Nagy, 1988).

How the Brain Builds Vocabulary

The brain first recognizes the sensory input from seeing, hearing,
and visualizing in separate but interrelated regions. These sensory response centers connect to higher cortical function for the
manipulation of words. It is this active processing (doing things
with words, from acting them out to creating graphic organizers)
that brings students ownership of the new vocabulary. In neurological terms, that ownership means the creation of new links in
the neuron network that connect the new words to similar words
in a patterning and categorization process that will be described in
more detail later.

Each of these neural networks can be constructed and activated
by vocabulary building. Strategies will be described to enhance
the brain's vocabulary processing through learning style strengths,
relating to existing storage categories, engagement (resonance),

and multisensory learning. Functional MRI and PET scan research combined with cognitive testing led me to seek, modify, and develop classroom strategies designed to build vocabulary learning compatible with my understanding of brain patterning and information consolidation. The strategies I have found successful are ones I believe promote active processing of vocabulary knowledge through manipulation in executive functioning and connection to categories and relational memories.

Vocabulary building is a microcosm of the larger process of literacy building. Just as the brain's cortical processing at the early stages of learning to read is not the same as the cortical processing of the skilled reader, learning vocabulary building strategies modifies brain functions in systematic, predictable ways as enriched vocabulary becomes evident in reading comprehension, verbal language, and writing (Sandak & Poldrack, 2004).

The Three Rs of Vocabulary

I break down vocabulary building into three components that work in sequence and in parallel to improve brain efficiency and build vocabulary success. Consequently, I developed or modified strategies appropriate for each aspect of vocabulary building. After describing these components of my vocabulary instruction I will offer the strategies I use to *resonate, reinforce,* and *rehearse.*

The guiding principal is to keep students engaged and motivated throughout vocabulary instruction as they build the skills and strong vocabulary that will give them access to meaning in print and richness in expressive language.

Resonate

To maintain attention, students must be engaged in the activity and must not have sensory input to the brain's processing centers blocked by the affective filter in the amygdala. The goal is to motivate students to attend closely to the sensory input of the pertinent information. To keep their stress down and allow the input of the sensory data to reach the rest of the brain, I use strategies aimed at helping students build competence and confidence. I want students to experience success and mastery and to see themselves moving toward goals they want to achieve. I strive to emphasize the value of specific vocabulary in whatever special interest areas students are motivated to learn about. To do this I survey their interests and bring in suitable reading material such as magazines about scuba diving, model airplanes, and computers. I have students work with partners with similar interests to construct lists of specialty vocabulary words that are found in magazines focused on topics that interest them. My purpose is to help students see vocabulary building practice as an intrinsically valuable, desired, achievable goal. If the challenge level is too high or interest level is too low, students tend to lose focus and learning comes to a stop. Once the students are invested in the goal, they are more motivated to do the work and stay on task to achieve the vocabulary they desire.

Reinforce

Vocabulary learning, like any desired knowledge-building behavior, must be reinforced in a rewarding manner to maintain motivation. Reinforcement strategies I find to be most successful are those that incorporate ongoing assessment and corrective feedback along with positive reinforcement.

Rehearse

Repetitive use of the learned vocabulary needs to be sustained for the knowledge to go from short-term or working memory to long-term memory storage, from where it can be readily accessed for future use. These rehearsals need to be sustained over time so consistent patterns of neuronal activation occur repetitively, strengthening the networks that link vocabulary in brain storage centers to the processing centers of higher cognition.

Resonate Through Motivation

People who have large vocabularies tend to be intrigued by words. To build students' motivation to put effort into their individually meaningful goals of vocabulary acquisition I seek strategies that resonate with their interests and learning style preferences. Although it helps all students to experience the benefits of building their vocabularies, consider your students as individuals and seek to help them develop their own personally meaningful goals that will motivate them to make the effort required to build their vocabularies. Consider the following goals, and add more of your own as you find motivators that resonate with students to help them recognize and internalize the personal value of vocabulary enhancement.

Interest: Students interested in writing, speaking, leadership, politics, management, business development, education, or communication will be motivated when they experience that learning specialty words gives them voice—the ability to describe and learn about the world in which they live.

Analytical Learners: Analytical students might appreciate the increased power that enriched vocabulary gives them to understand things about which they read, think, debate, and problem solve.

Individual Connections: You can build vocabulary interest by helping students be more aware of words in their everyday life as well as in their special interests. A basketball by itself is fun to bounce for a while, but when children see all the things experienced basketball players can do with that ball such as dribbling, passing, and throwing it into a basket in an exciting, interactive game, their motivation for acquiring basketball skills increases. When they are given instruction in the strategies and opportunities to practice the skills that build their successful manipulation of that basketball it becomes much more than a big ball to bounce. When they experience the satisfaction that comes from seeing their practice pay off in greater skill and success, they are motivated to continue to practice because they have felt the pleasure of becoming basketball players.

Motivating Literature: Just as having a basketball alone is unlikely to build motivation for skill building, neither are repetitive drills of passing and throwing likely to motivate practice if students don't have the awareness of the big picture—what a real basketball game looks like and feels like. Similarly, vocabulary instruction that focuses on repetitive, uninspiring skills, such as looking up definitions in a dictionary, is not going to result in students setting intrinsically motivated goals to mechanically study words.

When students develop an interest and awareness in words beyond formal vocabulary lists they are on the path to "playing real basketball" because they have a basket to aim at—a basket of words in a vocabulary repertoire they want to own. To continue the basketball analogy, once children see the big picture of basketball they are more interested in the sports page or biographies of favorite players. When students are inspired through motivating literature and learning activities they value as helping them achieve the goal of filling their word baskets, they will be responsive to paying attention to the words they see, hear, and use.

Motivated students are more likely to take more notice of words whose meanings they do not know, use strategies to understand challenging words, and recognize relationships between words. Interest and curiosity lead to the practices that build the neuronal circuits that bring students brain ownership of the new words.

Lower the Affective Filter and Raise the Resonance

Stress blocks learning. Krashen and others used the term affective filter to describe the phenomenon noted when students under high stress are not responsive to processing, learning, and storing new information (Krashen, 1989).

The neuroimaging visualization of the affective filters represents objective physical evidence that during periods of high stress, new learning just doesn't get in to the cognitive information processing networks of the brain. During vocabulary, as well as in any instruction, students need to be within the comfort zone achieved when they are engaged and not threatened by lessons. For vocabulary instruction to resonate with students emotionally and be processed cognitively we need to be dedicated observers of students and make needed adjustments to teach with goal-directed, achievable challenge. Strategies need to incorporate ongoing assessment to provide specific, corrective feedback. Vocabulary instruction that creates opportunities for discovery learning in students' ZPDs without the students hitting walls of frustration or resentment can reduce the information-blocking power of the affective filter (Routman, 2000).

Preventing overactivation of the amygdala is achieved by protecting students from aversive experiences that would block the passage of new information into the rest of the brain (Pawlak, Magarinos, Melchor, McEwen, & Strickland, 2003). For example, rote vocabulary homework and drills that involve copying definitions from the dictionary often end up being handwriting practice and not brain stimulating active learning endeavors. These assignments can also be frustrating when dictionary work is done without scaffolding such that students don't know which definitions are correct. Long lists of vocabulary words that don't have personal relevance or resonate with a topic the student wants to know about are tedious and may be perceived as threatening, unachievable tasks.

These emotions raise the affective filter. Even if the word and definition make it through the affective filter after repetitive drill, the information can still be blocked from reaching higher cortical processing if the students don't actively interact with the words in motivating activities that use executive frontal lobe functions (personal manipulation with knowledge). Rarely will students remember the meanings of these new words beyond the test. Without active processing to actually own the words, the rote memories become just compartmentalized pieces of information that students briefly store in short-term memory, try to recall for a test, and soon forget (Introini-Collision, Miyazaki, & McGaugh, 1991).

Vocabulary lessons taught in a language that students don't understand without using TPR (total physical response with gesturing, pointing to objects, pantomime and other techniques to give them the scaffolding they need) can also raise their affective filters. When students don't understand important words in a story or a subject lesson, they become frustrated and tune out. If more and more unfamiliar words are used that students don't comprehend, the stress can become overpowering and lead to a helplessness connected to hopelessness. Preteaching vocabulary to small groups or letting English language learners work with partners who are proficient English speakers can lower affective filter stress during more challenging lessons, where students might give up if frustration is too high (Pawlak et al., 2003).

For instruction to resonate it also needs to avoid the other extreme where students already know the material and there is no challenge to stimulate authentic curiosity and engagement in lessons. Achievable challenge tunes the amygdala to the ideal state of activation that can enhance the speed and efficiency of information flowing through into the memory consolidation and storage areas of the brain. It is just the right balance of these emotional and intellectual opportunities, and the incorporation of students' own interests and curiosity into the vocabulary instruction that will motivate them to work toward greater understanding and connection with the words (McGaugh, McIntyre, & Power, 2002; Patrick, Skinner, & Connell, 1993).

Propel Vocabulary Through the Affective Filter

Encourage Participation, Not Perfection

When you ask students to generate examples, if someone comes up with a "wrong" answer, it can be used as "a good nonexample" to help clarify the meaning of a word. Remind students that learning is not about proving what they already know, but about asking questions to change what they don't know into what they do know.

Focus on Understanding Your Students

Focus on understanding what students are trying to say, then giving positive feedback that includes the most accurate parts of their words in addition to missing important information. This can build confidence and clarity. Interacting with students about words through conversation, reading the words in rich context, or playing word games are more amygdala-resonant ways of learning vocabulary words than over-correcting students, raising their affective filters, and inhibiting their willingness to participate. During a lesson about the water cycle that includes the new vocabulary words "evaporation," "condensation," and "precipitation," I have the class work in three groups, each of which becomes expert in one of these words. For a large class there can be two groups assigned the same word to keep groups smaller and promote more individual participation.

To start, I show the class a PowerPoint presentation showing oceans, lakes with water levels during times of drought and after rainy seasons, and a variety of rain and snow storms. The PowerPoint is not didactic in that it does not detail the water cycle, but the three vocabulary words are embedded in the context of the pictorial demonstrations. The video is one I created from Internet websites using *iMovie* software that lets me incorporate video and audio clips from the Internet and my own voice.

I give each group a formal definition of their word. After answering questions that students raise to clarify the definitions, I set them to work in their groups with the following instructions:

> Discuss how to define your assigned word with words you commonly use. Take the formal definition you have and put it into your own words. Create a presentation for the class using a chart or overhead projection page you design that shows what your word means. You can draw examples of how your word can be used in terms of the water cycle and in terms of other things. One example is how water vapor condenses on car windows when people are inside a warm car on a cold day. You can also put on a skit or dance that demonstrates the meaning of your word.

Examples of my students' work have included

- A condensation-precipitation dance of a cloud getting denser as students stood closer together until it finally burst into rain and the students separated and scattered around like falling raindrops.

- Posters showing evaporation from a teapot, evaporation of dew from leaves (with before and after pictures as the sun rose higher), and a collage of computer images of different types of precipitation—rain, fog, snow, sleet, hail.

Support Student Participation

Many students build their listening vocabulary before they are ready to speak. If students are reluctant to speak because they are afraid of making mistakes, ask questions that can be answered with a "yes or no" answer. As students begin to respond with one-word answers and receive approval and encouragement, they will become more confident about expanding their answers into complete sentences. If a lesson forces students to go beyond their comfort zones, the language load of the activities may be too high. The associated stress could cause a significant barrier to learning (Meyer, 2000).

English language learners do better when their culture is appreciated and they do not feel that they are being required to reject their cultures of origin in order to learn English. Modeling the use of culturally connected topics in student-expanded manipulation of new words can lower affective filters. If an English language learner has Spanish as his primary language and is culturally attuned to a Latin American country, he might be more responsive to learning the meaning of "altitude" if the word is used in reference to a mountain range he is familiar with from his native country. Slow, simple definitions and sentences that refer to concrete objects rather then abstract concepts will be easier for students to understand at first. Learning vocabulary is a fluid process, and more sophisticated forms of speech can be added as students' word understandings develop (Meyer, 2000).

Comprehensible Input

For students more challenged by the vocabulary and for some ELL students, vocabulary instruction can build up starting with words somewhat familiar to them. Krashen described *comprehensible input* as language that is at or slightly above the language level that a person can understand. Instruction with comprehensible input is considered an implicit process that is not done consciously. This technique allows words to be understood with the help of gestures or pointing and may increase students' engagement and reduce stress. Students Krashen described in a sheltered subject matter class were noted to acquire vocabulary through the process of learning academic subject matter through such comprehensible input even without specific language instruction (Krashen, 1989).

One form of comprehensible input that can be useful to ELLs is the *language bath*. During a *language bath*, the teacher talks about a subject including key vocabulary, pictures, gestures, and demonstrations. Without being expected to produce English orally, students are able to hear new content vocabulary used appropriately. Once primed in this manner to a state of comfort and resonance, the students are prepared to participate in a class brainstorm activity discussing the new word (Meyer, 2000).

Sequential Learning

Break down the word learning process. It may help some students to follow a sequence when learning new words. Some sequential learners may benefit by listening to comprehensible input for a while before they are asked to use the word. They may want to demonstrate an idea with a drawing before using it in a sentence. Other students may be more comfortable with reading and writing before speaking the new word. You can help students achieve the affective state of comfort by strengthening the skills and learning style preferences they have and encouraging, not forcing, movement along the sequence.

Check for Understanding

When students are confused about word meanings and are already in a state of stress, they are less likely to ask for help or respond to general questions addressed to the class such as, "Do you all understand that?" Students appear to use a different kind of thinking when they construct original patterns for information they are given. More active thinking and more accurate assessment of understanding can be gained by asking students to rephrase a definition or concept in their own words in writing or verbally to partners as you circulate around the room.

Music

Music may lower the affective filter for English language learners as they acquire new vocabulary words. Try playing popular, familiar, and well-enunciated songs in English that have useful vocabulary words. Repetitions of songs students enjoy are used to enhance word memory in foreign language classes, so why not use them to build English language vocabulary?

GRAY MATTER

As with all skills that build with practice, multiple exposures to vocabulary words using a variety of multisensory activities that include seeing, hearing, visualizing, and manipulating words in multiple contexts, alone and with classmates, can build students' abilities to own not only the words, but also the meaning of text. Skill building expands students' potentials to participate in rich verbal and written interactions and increases motivation and resonance to reading and vocabulary instruction. Instruction that resonates with multiple learning styles may add to the activation-stimulated growth of multiple learning and memory storage centers in the brain.

The two prevailing theories to developing the large vocabulary necessary to master English are the Input Hypothesis (indirect instruction) and

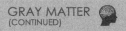

Output Hypothesis (direct instruction). Krashen is a proponent of the Input Hypothesis (IH) and implicit learning of vocabulary through reading and comprehensible input. For both first and second language learners of English, Krashen states that reading comprehensible input is the most valuable source of vocabulary acquisition (Krashen, 1989). In support of this hypothesis, Krashen believes that the more free reading time students have, the better they will score on vocabulary tests. During reading, students are likely to have some vagueness about unknown words that they encounter, but the Ouput Hypothesis (OH) asserts that it is not primarily context that builds comprehension, but rather repeated exposure to words embedded in interesting content that increases word knowledge. Critical to this process is not only the extent of the exposure to language, but also the individual's motivation toward the topic and text (Krashen, 1989). OH contends that people learn language by producing language. According to OH, verbal attempts that are successful will reinforce the language used, while unsuccessful attempts cause the speaker to alter his or her language in the future. The direct instruction supported by OH refers to explicit teaching of new word meanings with a skill-building method of learning vocabulary through deliberate methods and strategies from rote memory to analyzing word parts (Swain & Lapkin, 1995).

Proponents of explicit vocabulary instruction opine that vocabulary is mastered through practice and repetition. Therefore, vocabulary instruction should involve many opportunities to see and hear how words are used and to use, discuss, and relate new words with previously learned words. In addition, children are instructed in the use of resources such as glossaries, dictionaries, thesauri, and electronic and online resources. The direct instruction in explicit vocabulary teaching also includes the major construct of IH in that one of the strategies students learn is to use context to determine word meanings (but unlike IH, that is not the major form of learning).

Explicit vocabulary instruction targets at least two broad categories: unfamiliar words with high generalizability that are likely to recur in different contexts, and words necessary for understanding concept-specific content area words such as those that might be found in science textbooks. Word connotations are analyzed and practiced. For example, the words *revive* and *resuscitate* both mean to reawaken or revitalize, but *resuscitate* is often used in a medical context (restoring a comatose person to consciousness) and *revive* in the context of making something active, accepted, or popular again (revive swing dancing). Similarly, students are instructed in the different connotations of words; *cowardly* and *cautious* have related meanings but quite different connotations.

When the brain processes words through the OH intrinsic deduction process through reading, it is stressed that the text be engaging and motivating as well as at a level of difficulty that is sufficiently, but not overwhelmingly challenging. In that way, the experience of working to discover word meaning may resonate with students' desires for achievable challenge, and the data will pass unhindered through their affective filters into higher cortical functioning regions of the brain.

Instruction that resonates can be incorporated into explicit vocabulary instruction through the use of multisensory activities, instruction that connects with learning styles, and other factors—such as personal meaning, prior experience, real world relevance, and choice—that engage students' interest. When those qualities are developed in the teaching of individual words or vocabulary strategies, there is less reliance on rote memorization and more use of vocabulary instruction that engages and resonates actively with multiple brain centers.

Dopamine Fuels Resonance, Motivation, and Memory

Recall that information travels along the brain cells' branching and communicating sprouts (axons and dendrites) as electrical impulses. However, where these sprouting arms of one neuron connect to the next neuron in the circuit, the information has to travel across a gap between the end of one nerve and the beginning of the next one. In these synaptic gaps, there are no physical structures, like the wires that connect appliances to electric outlets, along which the electric impulses can travel. When crossing synapses, the information impulse must be temporarily converted from an electric one into a chemical one as it is carried by neurotransmitters across the synapse.

Dopamine, as described in the previous chapter, is an important neurotransmitter in the reading and word processing neural networks in the brain. Dopamine is also a major neurotransmitter for attention and executive function neuron networks that are found in the frontal lobes. Dopamine deficiencies in the frontal lobes have been associated with attention deficit hyperactivity disorder. One powerful trigger of dopamine release is pleasure. The pleasure-response theory of dopamine release describes the brain's release of dopamine during or in expectation of rewarding, pleasurable experiences. When learning activities induce pleasurable states in the brain, the dopamine released could be available to increase attention and focus (Black et al., 2002).

In addition, if learning activities are repeatedly linked to pleasurable experiences, students' brains may become conditioned to seek the pleasurable sensations that accompany dopamine release when they perceive a cue that the positively linked learning activity will begin (Montague, Hyman, & Cohen, 2004).

For example, if vocabulary lessons are associated with the fun and physical activity of acting out or drawing pictures of the meaning of the words, the students' brains may learn to associate the cue of the announced vocabulary lesson with the expectation of the reward of pleasant stimulation. The dopamine then released could enhance focus and executive function.

These are the lessons where I might act out the words and have students guess which one I am pantomiming from the list on the board. I also use an activity where I start sketching a representation of the word and students call out what word they think I am drawing from the word list.

Strategies to Promote Dopamine Release

Choice and Variety

Give students choices and variety in vocabulary building activities. Contributing to positive affect is student choice to pursue work of personal interest. Consider the enthusiasm of a science researcher on the brink of a discovery or an artist in the midst of a creative breakthrough. They are in zones of such focused attention that even basic needs such as hunger and sleep are ignored. Students may not reach that degree of intense connection to their vocabulary lessons, but they can come close.

Dopamine release could stimulate students to invest more attention in activities and lessons to which they feel an emotional and personal connection. Before introducing a new vocabulary unit for literature or technical words for other subjects, such as history or science, you can build excited anticipation in students by connecting the topic with a fun activity. Before a unit on percent, where I used banking to introduce the concepts of using percent to calculate interest, I give students blank checks, a check register, and deposit slips. I tell the students they will simulate using the money in their checking accounts to pay for items they want to buy. Students were encouraged to tell partners what things they want to purchase and why they are enthusiastic about having checking accounts similar to those they have seen their parents have.

I use words such as interest rate, deductions, deposits, checkbook register, withdrawal, account balance, and principle. These are also listed on a chart and copied into students' vocabulary journals. As students go through the process of starting with $100 in their accounts and adding $50 a week to their interest-bearing checking accounts, they make entries into their checking accounts and list the transactions using one of the appropriate terms from the vocabulary list. Student participate in a whole class discussion of what expenses they need to deduct from their checking accounts before they have a balance to spend on their desired items of purchase. Students make the deposits of $200 per month and deduct from that for rent, groceries, and utilities. They calculate how much interest they would earn after that money remained in the account one year if the account paid a simple interest of 5 percent a year.

Students then present their calculations with overhead projections of their checkbook registers and use the vocabulary words and the math to tell classmates what they have been saving for, how they have done so, and how many weeks they have needed to reach the desired account balance.

This activity is motivating and engaging with positive personal connections to build the dopamine-pleasure-attentive state. Such thinking appears to help build their intuitive understanding of the vocabulary words. Students participate with enthusiasm and focus to prepare their presentations. Some bring in pictures of the items they are saving for and classmates are encouraged to ask the speaker questions using the list of vocabulary words.

Assessments are based on presentations, the written material in students' checkbooks, overhead projector notes, and formal math problem tests. Formal assessment includes a vocabulary test where students use the words from the list to write sentences that describe their own checkbook projects.

Link Words to Personal Experiences and Interests

In one unit, we study adjectives found in a book we will soon read about colonial life. These include adjectives used in colonial times but not in common use in modern English. The students are asked to write diary entries as if they are children living in the colonies and to describe things they are interested in that correlate with their current interests. Sentences are to include the adjectives from the preview vocabulary list. Student-generated sentences include: "Her *courtly* manner encouraged me to taste the unfamiliar foods, such as scones and apple brown Betty that she served for dinner."

"Although he was a *contrary* person he was obligingly courteous when he joined me in a game of darts."

Try stimulating curiosity with a provocative question and discussion to heighten interest. When students develop interest in the topic or story to which the new words increase access, they may be in a dopamine-releasing pleasure state. Students are interested in how things impact them, especially when they predict a positive outcome, such that dopamine-reward release of the neurotransmitter is likely.

Before a unit about the ocean I ask global questions to prompt engagement in the topic of oceans.

- What would the world be like without oceans?
- What would you miss if there were no oceans?
- What is your favorite ocean animal and how do you think it could adapt to life on dry land?

As students respond to these questions I write down the words they use that will be likely to come up during our ocean-themed lessons. When they use words that could be replaced by more scientific terms I respond to their comments by reciting their statements back to them, substituting the vocabulary word for their word.

Student: I would miss the crabs and lobsters I like to eat.

Teacher: Yes, *crustaceans* make tasty meals.

Student: Without oceans the water would all be flat and the levels wouldn't change.

Teacher: I imagine that there would not be the changing water levels we see now, as *tides* change the water level of the oceans.

With well-constructed lessons, the released dopamine could do more than increase students' pleasure response. Because dopamine is such a prominent neurotransmitter in the prefrontal lobe organization and executive function centers, its release could also open or activate the brain pathways and circuits that carry information from superficial awareness into relational memory. Bottom line, if vocabulary instruction is enhanced with activities that the brain finds pleasant, the brain could be responsive to cues by making predictions and adjusting students' behaviors to achieve the pleasurable state it predicts. Imagine having students at a heightened state of attentive readiness when they see a new vocabulary list on the board! Lessons that resonate are more likely to pass efficiently through the affective filter and potentiate dopamine release. Vocabulary instruction designed with dopamine release and affective filter resonance in mind has the potential to build students' vocabulary skills, confidence, and knowledge access.

High-Frequency Words

A little bit of knowledge can go a long way when the knowledge is particularly useful. It may not seem like a great achievement to learn twenty-five words of a foreign language, but if you've ever traveled to a foreign country knowing how to ask for the restaurant, hotel, museum, beach, restroom, hospital, railroad station, and perhaps the names of a few items of food, you know how that small vocabulary was as useful as your passport. Your sense of comfort and well being was increased because you could communicate about your basic needs and priority interests.

Similarly, when students master grade-appropriate high frequency "sight words" they too can have the comfort, well-being, and hopefully the dopamine-pleasure response because they have access to much of the meaning in grade level books. That confidence helps them approach the new words without their affective filters overstressed so they can connect the strategies they have learned, such as contextual cues, to discern even the unfamiliar words.

I am no fan of rote memorization when it only serves the purpose of learning personally insignificant data for a test. Yet when it comes to studying the high-frequency words, I'm in favor of any technique that works, even repetitious and tedious drill, because the payoff is so great and the words won't be forgotten because they are reviewed so frequently in context. Those words will open many sentences and give students the access they need for reading to resonate with them as a pleasurable, nonthreatening experience.

In 1848, Edward Dolch wrote *Problems in Reading*, where he listed 220 high frequency words that have stood the test of time. These functionally important words account for over 50 percent of all the words students encounter in written material through 9th grade (Stahl, 1999). Using flashcards, class posters, and any other type of exposure that works, from songs to pantomime, these words once mastered should be instantly recognized in the context of reading them in text. The high-frequency words are the keys to the kingdom, and once students possess these keys, they will have the boost of motivation and confidence to persevere with the goal of building the more extensive vocabulary that opens a wider world of reading for pleasure and knowledge acquisition.

Prereading Preview of Vocabulary Words

To keep literature and vocabulary positive experiences that resonate and allow learning to pass unhindered through the affective filter, a variety of strategies are available for preteaching words from books to be read aloud. The general theme of these strategies is to provide students with the meanings of key words that will be used in the story. I do not expect students to fully grasp the meanings of these words during the introductory experiences. I emphasize these words to make it easier for students to identify the vocabulary I chose to target for their long-term memory retention.

Students have opportunities to mentally manipulate these words before the story is read through a variety of activities that result in students creating their own definitions of key words so their connections to the story's flow will not be broken when the word is read.

GRAY MATTER

Before considering brain-compatible strategies for this word preview process, consider the value of previewing. One analysis of teaching time found teachers spent an average of only 1.67 minutes on vocabulary during each reading lesson hour (Juel, 2006).

Naming of words is one of the specific cognitive processes involved in phonological skills and word processing. Images from fMRIs have defined a brain area of increased metabolic activity during phonological naming. This region is just in front of the area of frontal lobe most metabolically active during some phonological awareness activities, such as when phonological codes are retrieved from long-term storage (Aron, Gluck, & Poldrack, 2004; Poldrack et al., 2001).

To increase this brain activation, it follows that helping early readers connect new words to codes stored in memory could be increased by preteaching through multisensory activities that include visual, auditory, and writing activities to resonate with the different learning styles of children.

To keep students engaged in the word preview, consider selecting words that are most critical to understanding the text. To keep the number of pretaught words to a minimum, words that are the specific names of members of a known category can be left for students to connect with the storage categories they already have in long-term memory. For example, if the text mentions a food, and it can be inferred through contextual clues that the word refers to a type of food, students can connect the new word with the known category on their own. However, words that should be pretaught are those that are critical for understanding the meaning of the text, appear frequently throughout a text, are important terminology for understanding the text or content (and that are not explained within the text), and words that students will encounter often in their future reading or discussions (Roit, 2002).

Strategies for Word Preview

Connecting with Prior Knowledge

Prompting children to think about situations in their lives that relate to a new word is likely to increase the chances that they will recall and use the word when appropriate circumstances occur as the result of building a relational memory.

Teacher: When you find out you will do something you really love, like go to the zoo or play soccer, you might say you are *excited* but you could also say you are *enthusiastic*. When else could you say you are *enthusiastic*?"

Student: Before my birthday party.

Personal Connections Resonate
Through Cultural Background

If the new word can be connected to personally meaningful experiences, such as cultural background, there may be an existing category in memory storage to link with the new word. When that linkage is strengthened by positive emotional connections to that memory, the relational memory that is built around the new word could link it to a strong, accessible neuronal memory circuit.

If the new word is "appetite," the connections can be made to children of different cultural backgrounds with a discussion of which food aromas or smells (embedding the synonym, *aromas*, for *smells* adds exposure to yet another sophisticated word) give them a big *appetite* or desire for that food.

The other reason to add resonance through cultural context is to review planned reading material for common words in English that may be unfamiliar concepts to ELLs. Students' lack of background experience can add to the intimidation some students feel when learning English as a second language. Background knowledge required by a text is a powerful variable in reading comprehension for both English and non-English speakers (Peregoy & Boyle, 2005).

If the word is "president" and some ELLs are from countries without presidents and are not familiar with the concept of the American president, they can be exposed to the culturally novel word by asking them if they have been in a classroom or club where there was a president. If students are unfamiliar with any type of club president, the discussion can start with team captains and what they do for the team. That can be followed by a discussion of what a class captain could do for a class. Next would be a comparison of team captain to class president and ultimately to a country's president. Students from other countries could then be the "experts" if they can explain what the word is for "captain" or "president" in their country of heritage or birth and first language.

GRAY MATTER

Cultural load can be a major barrier to English language learning if the knowledge required is not explicitly explained in order for the learner to accurately comprehend the meanings of a story or learning activity in English (Meyer, 2000). It is the cultural load of a lesson that can make vocabulary learning of a seemingly simple word like "water" so difficult that comprehension of the story or lesson is limited and affective filters restrict new learning of not only the word, but the rest of the lesson.

It may even be necessary to consider the cultural significance of the word for children who grew up in other countries. Culturally diverse students may look at the same information with very different lenses that may cause the information to be confusing, disturbing, and at times even offensive. If a student comes from a country where water is carried from the river or pumped from a well, a pantomime of turning on a faucet would have little meaning. Further, if a child's culture reveres water as sacred, they might misinterpret pouring water into a cup as the demonstration of something religious. When a particular book or unit will have a high cultural load consider doing more than previewing words with pantomime or illustrations. These lessons can be opportunities to engage all learners through first-hand experiences such as experiments, field trips, class speakers (parents or community members), manipulatives, and cross-curricular lessons. When teachers lighten students' cultural loads, students feel more comfortable expressing their confusion so vocabulary preview can be adapted accordingly (Meyer, 2000).

Relating Vocabulary Words to Categories

The neuroimaging and qEEG studies provide data that appear to support cognitive research and the experience of classroom teachers who find it is easier for students to learn related words than unrelated words. Considering that the brain works by pattern detecting, relating, and storage to connect its 100 billion neurons, it is neuro-*logical* to help students discover (active deduction) or to demonstrate to them the clues that may help them connect incoming information with stored patterns or prior knowledge.

The brain naturally seeks to find patterns, make sense of information and experiences, and evaluate the personal and emotional significance of an event. It is therefore brain research-compatible to expedite vocabulary learning by teaching students to learn a group of words related to a single topic (navigation, body parts, action verbs) rather than the random group of vocabulary words sometimes included in some reading curriculum.

Students may retain the new information by activating their previously learned knowledge that relates to the new material. Assuming that prior knowledge exists in stored loops of brain cell connections (circuits of neurons connected by branching axons and dendrites) I have molded teaching strategies aimed at helping students recognize patterns and then make connections to process the new working memories so they can travel into the brain's long-term storage areas.

The activities I find most useful incorporate vocabulary and word meanings to other known words and ideas. Words appear to be remembered and recalled more easily when students' understanding of words is deepened and their semantic networks are widened. One explanation theorizes that when new words link with the patterning in the brain's neural networks they become incorporated into these networks (Stahl, 1999). When selecting preview vocabulary words before the class reads a book it seems consistent with the classification network arrangement of the brain to sort the words by commonalities that are made explicit to students. Consider giving students the opportunity to deduce the commonality through class discussion as they begin to learn the meanings of the words. For example, listing words such as sneaker, boot, sandal, and flip-flop can elicit the commonality of types of shoes.

Generally new vocabulary words found in literature or trade books on any subject have some contextual commonalities with each other. The use of rich thematic or subject related trade books and cross-curricular units can also have the advantage of building subject knowledge along with vocabulary as students explore and revisit the meanings and uses of words frequently repeated in such books and units of study. Because vocabulary development is significantly enhanced by the amount and variety of material children read, the introduction of trade books has additional value (Snow, Burns, & Griffin, 1998).

An example is a grade-level appropriate book about photosynthesis. When this is the class book, there will automatically be a group of related vocabulary words. When students learn the concept word "reaction" regarding the chemical reactions of converting sunlight to energy, this can be demonstrated by a simple chemical reaction such as the release of carbon dioxide when an *Alka Seltzer* tablet is dropped in a glass of water.

Students can make word lists or posters with examples of other types of reactions—such as heating water to make it boil, popping out of hiding and saying "boo!" to have another person react by being startled, or putting down the cat food and having the cat come into the kitchen.

Visual organizers, such as a tree and branch style, fit well in this activity. Students can include examples of chemical reactions (litmus paper changes color to acids and bases) and others could include types of reactions such as emotional reactions (laugher, crying), physical reactions (water heated to 212 degrees Fahrenheit boils), political reactions (a candidate who angers voters doesn't get elected), or societal reactions (a country that supported its neighbor after a tidal wave is assisted by that neighbor when its residents sustain severe crop losses).

Another opportunity to have vocabulary instruction through categories is when a teachable moment or special event prompts students' curiosity about a topic. If a class member breaks an arm and brings in the x-rays, that can prompt a discussion of bones and anatomy. Using classification, words can be grouped that fit into the circulatory system, respiratory system, musculo-skeletal system, nervous system, and digestive system.

Strategies for Brain Patterning of Vocabulary

Word learning strategies such as building analogies, similes, and metaphors connect with the brain patterning networks that appear most efficient at linking new information to existing categories of prior related knowledge. The following activities are the ones I use to help make explicit the relationships among meanings of words and give students the opportunity to actively manipulate new words in their cognitive processing.

Card Sorts

To scaffold students to recognize similarities or categories for new words, prompt them to consider what the word reminds them of and how they may have seen it used before (a science book chapter about weather or a history book about navigational exploration). After they understand the definition, they could develop relationships with prior knowledge categories when they think about

GRAY MATTER

Brain scans were carried out when subjects used visual imagery along with metaphors they created. Subjects were given a new word and its definition and asked to pair it with a word they already knew that had a similar meaning. The brain activity during this subject-created metaphor construction was used as a baseline. They were then asked to connect this metaphor pairing to a visual image. Subjects said that their images were more vivid when they connected the new words to metaphors and their scans showed increased areas of brain activation (Harris & Sipay, 1990). Studies like this support strategies using both visualization and relational categorization to connect new vocabulary to previous knowledge.

examples of the word. As they see relationships between familiar and less familiar terms, the meaning of the new vocabulary word may be remembered more efficiently through categories and relational memory.

Examples of word sort cards, where vocabulary is practiced and words are related by category, are words with similar prefixes, roots, or spelling patterns (words that end with -ate), or grouped by themes (transportation, emotions, things that are cold). This can be a self-correcting individual or learning center activity when cards with the same color on one side or the same design (some with stars, others with circles or squares drawn on the flip side) are the ones that fit in the same category. Students start with the cards all turned toward the printed words and after they sort them they flip the cards to see if all cards in each category have the same color. Self-correcting feedback comes from seeing the mismatched color.

Students Create Examples

Personal connections, prior knowledge, and student interest can all add to the neurological resonance of an experience and help propel the new data through the RAS and amygdala's affective filter. The example-making process is similar to the idiom and simile process in that it begins with teacher modeling of a vocabulary word, its definition, and the use of the word in a sentence where its meaning is embedded in the other words of the sentence.

I write: "*Temporary* means impermanent or not permanent." Then I say and write an example of correct use of the word: "The trailer was their *temporary* shelter when their house was being rebuilt after the fire."

When this strategy is used in a reading preview of vocabulary words, the definition I use is one that is appropriate for the word's use in the text we will read. (If our reading uses the word "bond" in reference to a binding or manacles, I will use that definition rather than the one pertaining to agreements or contracts.) After the reading of the word in the book, I subsequently discuss the alternate meanings of the word.

After my modeling, students connect with their interests and prior knowledge to create their own sentences, first the whole class, then individually or in pairs. In these examples, the students are required to also use a sentence where the definition of the word is embedded in the sentence.

When these sentences are shared and students explain their use of the word in their sentences, they are once again manipulating the word cognitively by thinking and verbalizing the relationship between their example sentence and the word. The goal is to restimulate the new network of relational memory.

When students practice writing functional definitions in their own words, the experience can resonate with their personal connections and enjoyment of selecting their own defining words. Students can enrich the activity to their individual achievable challenge levels by incorporating previously learned vocabulary words in their personal definitions. (As a general policy I encourage students to underline any former vocabulary word they use in subsequent writing activities for extra credit—otherwise I might not recognize them and acknowledge their effort.) With the personal manipulation of the word in their prefrontal cortex, my interpretation of the neuroimaging suggests that students are not just memorizing definitions that I provide. They are doing the active thinking and processing the word in their higher cognitive executive functions, so they have the opportunity to gain a deeper understanding and more permanent memory of the new word.

Strategies of Roots, Prefixes, and Suffixes

By the end of 2nd grade, children in the lowest vocabulary quartile have acquired slightly more than one root word a day over seven years for a total of about 3,000 root word meanings. Yet children in the highest quartile have acquired an average of three root words a day for a total of about 7,000 root word meanings (Biemiller, 2004).

As previously noted, students' neural filters appear to be more receptive to new information input that resonates with their comfort levels with achievable challenge. When text is beyond students' comprehension strategy levels, they often become disengaged with raised affective filters. These students appear to be less successful at higher cortical processing of the information. Instruction in the strategy of increasing vocabulary through recognition of word roots, prefixes, and suffixes can help students advance not only their vocabulary, but also their levels of reading.

The use of prefixes, roots, and suffixes was described in Chapter 2 with reference to patterning. When vocabulary instruction is integrated with discussion of common prefixes, suffixes, or roots, there is the advantage that students can connect future new words with stored memory relational categories to recognize familiarity in the new word and connect prior knowledge to assess the new word. If students know the prefix "ped" and have a memory category of words that include "ped" such as "pedestrian" and "peddle" they may connect with that memory category when they see or hear a new related word such as "peddler" (from the historical reference that the first sales people walked to their customers or to bring their goods to public markets). Students now have the opportunity to retrieve knowledge from that category and build a relational memory with the new word.

An activity to engage prior knowledge is to encourage generating other words with a root, suffix, or prefix in a vocabulary word being studied. From the list of words students generate, they are prompted to mentally manipulate the information by deducing what the commonality is in the repeated root, suffix, or prefix. When they deduce that "ped" has something to do with foot, their relational memories connect to the new word and their opportunities for future word identification may grow along with the dopamine releasing satisfaction of discovery.

Visualization for Vocabulary Retention

Building a mental model may transform new ideas and information into a pattern that can be added to memory, where it can endure as knowledge that can be retrieved in the future. When students build a mental model, the information they form into a pattern appears to be consistent with the way the brain processes sensory input. As such, visualization of word meanings as mental pictures could facilitate connections to their stored, patterned prior knowledge. The new information could then have greater potential to be retained.

Illustrations

With the knowledge of the potential value of patterning and relational memories for the learning of new information, seeing visual representations could increase comprehension and retention of new vocabulary words. To make knowledge of the word a multisensory experience, consider including illustrations, photographs, computer images, and videos where the word is acted out—as on *Sesame Street*—allowing students to encounter the information through both sound and sight.

When using pictures, it helps to show a variety of images that represent a certain word or concept to keep conceptualization clear.

For example, when the word is "soft," if only an illustration of a pillow is used, students may think the word "soft" means "pillow" or refers only to the softness of a pillow. This can result in incorrect classification categories that could become confusing later when the category is stimulated by a word to which it is not truly related. Showing multiple examples of soft things such as bunnies, velvet, and cotton balls can eliminate this confusion. The duplication using multiple images can also be likely to resonate with more students who have categories of prior knowledge for at least one of the images shown. For other students, the redundancy might stimulate more neural cross-connections and reactivate existing neural networks to potentially make them stronger and easier to reactivate for future recall.

Individual Visualizing

When students are prompted (after modeling) to visualize their own example of the meaning of a word, they have another opportunity to actively manipulate the word mentally. After giving imagination free reign, more of students' brains may be engaged if they put their visualization into words, diagrams, or pictures. They can describe their images to each other, write them in words, or draw sketches. Just as athletes may visualize a move before they execute it, students can be encouraged to visualize the word, especially related to a physical action, to create more cortical cross-connections. When they draw diagrams, create models, and engage their sight, hearing, touch, or movement, they are making connections between the new information and something they already know. They are engaging multiple brain pathways and increasing the likelihood of memory storage and effective retrieval.

The more bizarre the visual image, the more memorable it becomes. Modeling becomes valuable here to show students how visualization can be used for vocabulary words. For an example, I have described my visualization of the word "hypotenuse" as I illustrate my visualization on the board. I explain that the diagram is not always necessary but I am using it to illustrate what my brain is visualizing. I say, "I imagine a *high* hangman's gallows, built with a right angle, with a pot in a *noose* hanging from the gallows. This helps me remember the word "hypotenuse" and the position of the *hy-pot-en-use* in a right triangle."

This visualization process can include humor, creativity, pleasure, and self-satisfaction. All of these predispose the limbic system to add emotional power as it passes the image and the attached concept through the amygdala, left prefrontal lobe, hippocampus, and on into long-term memory storage. In addition to generating mental images, if kinesthetic activity can be incorporated, the student may have at least two different memory circuits activated. I have used visual images accompanied by a sketch on the board for unfamiliar terms, but one always elicits groans and giggles, and is so well remembered that new students come to my class asking when I'm going to teach them about polygons. Similarly, former students come back and tell me they never forgot that math vocabulary word. For the explanation of *open* compared to *closed* polygons, I draw a closed multisided polygon with a bird inside. I then open the polygon by erasing a portion of one of the sides. I next erase the bird and say, "When the polygon is open, *Polly* is *gone*."

Even with highly conceptual, subject specific terms in history or science, if the students can actively do something with the new vocabulary word, they can ultimately own it and store it in permanent memory. The more abstract the information, the more creative you need to be to help students relate the material to personal experiences or consider its practical or future applications.

I have used visualization activities to promote student mental manipulation of words that are especially conceptual in science, math, and social studies. I have volunteers draw pictures of the word and visualization that we post on the bulletin board. Samples of student work have included

• "Camouflage" where the student camouflaged the letters of the word by blending them into background colors and patterns.

• "Diameter" where a student drew a sickly (*dying*) looking *meter* stick as the *dying meter* or *diameter* of a circle.

• "Embargo" was depicted with a jail cell with bars. The letter pair "Em" was constructed to be like two letters who were trying to get into the jail cell but were kept out by the bars. *Em* couldn't pass the *bar*s to *go* into the cell.

Personalizing

When students personalize vocabulary words they may further activate the areas of the brain that help form memories. Consider helping students connect the word with as many senses as possible to build stronger memory circuits.

For example, after learning the definition of an "electron," students visualize an electron orbiting the nucleus of an atom, mimic the buzz of electricity as it whizzes by, or feel a tingling associated with the electron's negative charge by rubbing a balloon against their arms and feeling their hair move. If they then draw a sketch of their visualizations and verbally communicate them to partners, or write about them in their own words, multiple brain pathways may be stimulated to carry the new information into long-term memory. The theory would be that because they have personalized the information, their amygdalas could be more likely to select this sensory information to attend to and pass along to the left prefrontal cortex.

Another example came from a middle school class I taught where students considered the meaning of ethics and ethical dilemmas in a cross-curricular unit. Students had the opportunity to go to deeper levels of visualization embedded with emotional components by personalizing selected vocabulary concept words. They were asked to consider ethical dilemmas students might face today. Cross-curricular relationships were included as students connected the concept of ethical dilemma with the dilemmas of the non-Jews during the Holocaust who struggled with risks to their own families to hide Jews from Nazis in the books, *Number the Stars* and *The Diary of Anne Frank.*

To further process the concept of "ethical dilemma" through personalization and stimulation of executive functions such as judgment and comparison, I asked them to think of an ethical dilemma that could happen today. If students didn't come up with one, I had one to supply: "What if your neighbor was hurting his dog and you saw him do it again and again. What if he saw you watching him and told you he would poison your dog if you reported him. What would you do? How would you feel" When children considered how they would respond and made a mental movie of the imagined experience, words related to ethics and ethical dilemmas took on personal meaning and may have become stronger relational memories.

Graphic Organizers

Concept definition maps and graphic organizers with illustrations can help students engage cognitively with new vocabulary words.

• Student groups can make their own flashcards of new vocabulary featuring illustrations or computer/magazine examples of the words and share these flashcards with other groups.

• Word maps organized as tree and branches or planets orbiting the sun can have the vocabulary word in the center surrounded by lists of synonyms, antonyms, multiple definitions, and sentences using the word. This can be started in class and completed for homework instead of the dreaded task of looking up the word in the dictionary.

• When words are conceptually challenging, concept definition maps can be provided. Students put the vocabulary word in the center and fill in connecting bubbles where prompts are included such as: "What is it?" and "What is it like?" Students then fill in examples of the concept. For the word "rotation" in the "What is it?" circle or branch they could list synonyms or definitions such as "turning around" or "revolving." Under "What is it like?" they can write "planets rotating" or "classroom jobs rotating."

• More advanced concept maps could include branches for synonyms, antonyms, roots, sketches, translation into a second language, multiple meanings, and information about the historical origin and development of the word.

• Cloze sentences can be used as assessment and as a way of teaching or reviewing vocabulary. A sentence, with strong contextual support, has the vocabulary word deleted. Students brainstorm possible replacements. Engagement is possible because there is not a single answer, so multiple students in a small group can generate multiple synonyms.

Getting in *Touch* with Words

Real Objects and Realia

When you are teaching students about a concrete item, an effective teaching strategy is to show them an actual item (triangle, insect, telescope). If that isn't possible, realia (a toy version of a real object) can be used (toy car, model dinosaur). To increase the sensory experience, students enjoy exploring objects with all of their relevant senses.

Physical Movement Pumps Up Vocabulary

If I am short of lesson time for vocabulary words, I act them out myself and have students select the word from a list on the board that matches my pantomime. Other times I ask students to make a physical response that reminds them of the word.

To create lasting reminders of physical movements for words, I have a class photo taken and ask all the student to pose with a "haughty" expression. I prompt them by saying they should think of the expression a rude king or queen makes after being served tea in a dirty cup by an unwashed servant. I have created bulletin board displays of such photos for the units we are studying and periodically put up a display of a previous vocabulary list and the associated photos as a memory reinforcer or a match game at a work station.

Vocabulary-Rich Speaking

Young children's listening and speaking competence is in advance of their reading and writing competence. They understand more words spoken in context than they can read independently. As children are developing their reading and writing competence, words richly used in the classroom with contextual clues can expand their verbal vocabulary. That auditory knowledge will be a ZPD into which their reading and writing vocabulary can grow.

Word-rich classrooms are ones where teachers use sophisticated words in comprehensible context or with realia, pantomime, illustrations, or TPR (total physical response). These words can be used in questions such that students are encouraged to repeat the word in their responses. For example: "What are three ways you might notice if a person had just received *alarming* news?" "What are three things an *obstinate* person might say?" "What are three things that would *aggravate* you?" Doing this while the student has the meaning available gives them the opportunity to process the meaning instead of guessing at an answer (adapted from Beck & McKeown, 2003).

Students can also be encouraged to elaborate on the words they use. When they use noninformative, unspecific, slang words such as "stuff" or "that thingy" it is reasonable to stipulate that in the interest of more sophisticated class conversations they should find a more informative word to substitute for the slang. Students can ask classmates for suggestions and soon it becomes an enjoyable class ritual to "find the sophisticated word."

When multiple methodologies are used for teaching vocabulary, students have multiple opportunities to interact with words and reading through activities that resonate with their interests, prior knowledge, and learning style preferences in neuro-*logical* ways.

Vocabulary instruction that incorporates multiple opportunities to learn and practice the words and the vocabulary building and comprehending strategies can give students more power to access the riches of the reading kingdom.

Reinforce and Review

GRAY MATTER

Working memory, or short-term memory, involves the ability to hold and manipulate information for use in the immediate future. Information is only held in working memory for about 20 seconds. The challenge students face is to move information from their working memories into their long-term memories. If they don't do this in about the first few minutes after receiving the information, that information can be lost. (Think about the last time someone gave you driving directions, which seemed so clear when you heard them but were lost to you once you made the second right turn.) To keep this newly learned material from slipping away, it needs to enter the network of the brain's wiring.

After repeated practice, working memories are set down as permanent neuronal circuits of axons and dendrites ready to be activated when the information is needed. When a memory has been recalled often, its neuronal circuits are more highly developed because of their repeated activation. (As noted previously, cells that fire together, wire together.) When neurons repeatedly fire in sync with one another, they are more likely to form inter-neuron connections. As the connections grow stronger by repeated stimulation, a given neuron becomes more likely to trigger another connected neuron (Chugani, 1998).

Like exercising a muscle, these circuits then become more efficient and easier to access and activate. Practice results in repeated stimulation of the memory circuit. Like hikers along a trail who eventually carve out a depression in the road, repeated practice stimulates cells in the memory circuit such that the circuit is reinforced and becomes stronger. This means it can be quickly turned from off to on, and switched on through a variety of cues coming in from the senses.

GRAY MATTER

Brain-mapping studies have allowed scientists to track what parts of the brain are active when a person is processing information. The levels of activation in particular brain regions have been associated with which facts and events will be remembered. For example, an fMRI study that focused on visual memory had subjects placed in an fMRI scanner view and then re-view a series of pictures. The researchers found that activity levels in the prefrontal cortex and a specific area of the hippocampus correlated with how well a particular visual experience was encoded and how well it was remembered (Gabrieli & Preston, 2003).

A study that focused on verbal memory had subjects try to remember words, either by their meaning or by their appearance (upper- or lowercase spelling). Again, activity levels in the prefrontal cortex (on the left where the Broca's language center is for over 90 percent of people) and the same parahippocampal area predicted which words were remembered or forgotten in subsequent tests. The researchers discovered that words were much more likely to be remembered when subjects concentrated on semantics (meaning), rather than on their appearance (Wagner et al., 1998).

These examples of how neuroimaging can directly give evidence of what happens in the brain during learning and review led me to use strategies involving active cognition (student manipulation of words) to increase vocabulary and other memory learning.

Reinforcement of Vocabulary After the Story

After a story has been read and discussed the vocabulary words can be contextualized as they were used in the story and then beyond. If a story used the word "ignore" students can be reminded that, "Bob ignored his mother's advice and climbed the tree" was a sentence from the book.

Students can review the definition, and the word usage can be reinforced by questions that also use the word "ignore" and prompt the students to use it in their response. When asked, "Did you ever ignore anything?" students have answered from personal experience: "I ignore my baby brother when he screams" or "I ignore the telephone ringing when I don't want to talk to anybody." After a book is completed, students who finish other assignments early can take a word from the word list and create a page for it in the class dictionary of "Words We Know" including a preapproved definition, sentence, and illustration or drawing. Advanced word pages can include a listing of other definitions for the word and sample sentences for these alternative definitions.

Review

Applying Previously Learned Words to New Stories

It is reinforcing and resonating when students can share their success at finding previously studied words in new contexts or subsequent stories. This activity can be taken a step further when students have the opportunity to look for places where previously learned words can be substituted for a less sophisticated word. This achievable challenge can include all students because words that resonate in the memory of some students may not be recalled as efficiently in classmates. For example, a tactile learner who connected with the word "locomotive" when realia was used in the learning of that word might be the one who volunteers "locomotive" as a sophisticated word to replace the word "train" in a new story. A visual or analytical learner may be the student to recall the word "transcontinental" from the prefix "trans" word list and suggest "transcontinental" as a sophisticated substitute for "cross-country."

Using Words Outside the Book

Frequent encounters with new words help them become permanent. Posting the previous story's vocabulary words on a bulletin board next to the book cover can be a reminder to students to use these words in their speaking and writing.

Fun class responses can be designated such that when students hear one of the posted words, they quietly put their thumbs up and make notes to themselves. When there is an appropriate break in the lesson, students who wrote down the word can report its use and meaning and drop a marble in the class party jar.

When students begin to intentionally use the previously studied vocabulary words to see if their classmates notice and raise their thumbs, so much the better as evidence that students are incorporating these words into their oral vocabularies.

An extension of the classroom word search takes it outside the classroom to the students' independent reading and exposure to oral language. If they write down a vocabulary word they hear or read outside class and bring it in on a card, including the sentence and context in which it was heard, it can also be reported and valued as a marble for the class jar.

Word Treasure Chest

A box containing cards with previously learned words on one side and definitions on the other can be available for students to review on their own. When a table's group members are due for recognition, they can take the word treasure box, select the words, and call on classmates who volunteer to give the definition or use the word in an illustrative sentence.

Another use for the words in the treasure chest is to play a classroom version of the commercial game *Pictionary*, which involves students selecting a word from the chest and sketching a representation of it on the board. Students can work in teams or as a whole class to name the word being represented by the sketch.

Deal or No Deal

This review activity uses the name of a television game show. I select a word from the word treasure chest or from my ongoing list for which I have realia, objects, or illustrations to match the word. I write and say the word and show the class the object or picture. They hold thumbs up for "deal," meaning yes the two are a match, or thumbs down for "no deal" or no match. When there is no match, I immediately hold up the correct match to reinforce the correct relationship in their memories.

Same Time Last Year

I save digital photos on my computer of students from previous years demonstrating the words we studied then. The photographed students are excited because they enjoy having their picture taken to "teach" next year's students. When we get to the same words the following year, I project the students with the "haughty" expressions or muscles "flexed" in their arms, and the current students enjoy matching these portrayals with the listed vocabulary words. Here we have personal relevance and familiarity (with the students a year ahead of them in school) to build resonance to the activity.

When our class is ready for a review a few months later, the current year's students have the chance to model the word. I take a few photos to add to my photo word archive. Activities like these stimulate multiple brain regions—physical, visual, and auditory—and the peer modeling from the older students adds status to the vocabulary word.

Vocabulary Review Homework

To rehearse words learned in class, students can enjoy the motivation of choice in how they will review the word at home. Options include using a certain number of the words in a poem, story, song, commercial, or slogan. When volunteers perform or read their assignments, classmates connect with hearing "their" words used by the volunteer classmate in a different format. This can be the type of pleasurable reinforcement experience that stimulates their brains' dopamine.

Alternative homework lets students be the teachers as they make up match tests using the key words. On one side of the page they list the words, and on the other they create sentences with a blank space for one of the match words to be filled in. Students can switch tests and review answers with partners (after they have been checked for accuracy). To make the activity more rewarding, the best match sentences can be selected for a whole-class assessment, with acknowledgment given to the authors of the sentences chosen for excellent contextual use of the word.

Younger students or students needing accommodations for learning disabilities or English language learning might have more success using the puzzlemaker.com Web site, where they insert the word and a one-word definition and a crossword puzzle is created for them to practice with or trade with a classmate to practice in school.

Independent Reading

A powerful source of student acquisition of new words is through independent reading. This is not surprising, as the vocabulary content of books is far more varied than the vocabulary content of ordinary conversation, popular songs, or television dialogue.

However, independent reading alone, without student motivation to notice, rather than skip, all the new words they read, won't build vocabulary as much as an approach to reading where students become interested and enthusiastic about words so they want to know their meanings (Cunningham & Stanovich, 1998).

GRAY MATTER

To create confident and enthusiastic readers who gain meaning, pleasure, and knowledge from a variety of print materials, students benefit from extensive experience with language and literature.

Extensive reading gives students multiple exposures to words and allows them to see vocabulary in rich contexts. When students choose their books they are more likely to want to take the time to discover the meaning of unfamiliar words. The value of chosen independent reading ties into Krashen's belief that developing a large vocabulary is the necessary part of mastering a language that is most associated with *implicit learning* of vocabulary through reading. Krashen's Input Hypothesis (IH) described earlier contends that language is learned by understanding messages that are communicated to us, particularly through comprehensible input (language that is at or slightly above the language level that a person can understand). Acquiring language through taking in *comprehensible input* is an implicit process that is not done consciously. Indirect or implicit vocabulary acquisition occurs when students engage in extensive oral interactions with adults and peers and when they read and are read to. This implicit vocabulary learning increases the more widely they read and the more types of texts and media they are exposed to. For both first and second language learners of English, Krashen states that reading comprehensible input is the most valuable source of vocabulary acquisition (Krashen, 1989).

Stahl and Fairbanks (1986) reported that time spent reading, in school and at home, in a variety of genres, is correlated to the development of a strong vocabulary. Krashen goes so far as to say that pleasure reading is the best preparation students can have for the serious study of literature that awaits them in later school years. He contends that if students get sufficient opportunity to engage with low-risk reading, in which they will not be graded on their comprehension, students will read more and develop vocabularies and a love for reading that will support them when the time comes to read the classics (Krashen, 1989).

Middle School

Vocabulary takes another jump in middle school, as it is more difficult to comprehend expository text than narrative text and more of the required reading in middle and high school is expository text. This is also the time when students who have the ability to use and model increased vocabulary to express themselves in a more interesting and mature way may use more and more slang and nonverbal communication (postures and eye-rolls) or avoid class discussions in reaction to their perception of peer pressure against "smart kids" or "show offs."

Many students in middle school will need to be reminded, coaxed, and connected to vocabulary development through activities that resonate with their developmental stage. If students have difficulty using a rich vocabulary when they write, they can have an enjoyable class experience where they use a book thesaurus or computer thesaurus. There will be fun and giggles when they randomly select any of the multiple replacement words for their highlighted words. This exercise, when students are invited to read aloud their most bizarre word substitutions, will intrigue the class with thesaurus options. At first, the response might be to see how silly the substitutions can make their sentences. However, my students have found that after experimenting with the thesaurus, they eventually become more comfortable using it. They make more active discriminations among the word options and enrich their written and oral vocabulary with more sophisticated, colorful, and specific words that do make their sentences sound better.

Middle school and late elementary school years may be times when students are exposed to formal instruction in a foreign language. They begin to recognize common roots, and that awareness can be linked across the curriculum to explicit instruction in using common roots to identify new vocabulary words. In these connections they can benefit by direct instruction and review of lists of roots, common prefixes, and suffixes to figure out the meaning of new vocabulary words. This will also help English language learners incorporate their first language (if their language, such as Spanish, French, or Italian, has words with similar roots) into a systematic deduction of the meaning of new words they encounter in English.

Learning Promotes Learning

Engaging in the process of learning increases one's capacity to learn as demonstrated by neuroimaging studies of plasticity and rehearsal neuronal network stimulation described earlier. Each time a student participates in any endeavor, a certain number of neurons are activated. When the action is repeated, such as in a follow-up science lab experiment, rehearsing a song, or when the information is repeated in subsequent curriculum, scans suggest that the same neurons respond again. The more times one repeats an action (practice) or recalls the information, the more dendrites sprout to connect new memories to old (plasticity), and the more efficient the brain becomes in its ability to retrieve that memory or repeat that action.

Eventually, just triggering the beginning of the sequence results in the remaining pieces falling into place. This repetition-based sequencing is how we are able to do many daily activities almost without having to think about them, such as touch-typing or driving a car. The reason for this ability goes back to the construction and strengthening of those memory pathways in the brain.

Very few educators resort to having students learn only by rote memorization or limit instruction to only drill-and-kill worksheets day after day in hopes of imprinting vocabulary words in students'

brains. Teachers know from their own experiences how briefly
that material remains accessible to students. I have heard teachers
recall occasions when they inadvertently gave students a vocabulary
worksheet from a generic vocabulary workbook that the students
had already completed (not related to a book they read in class)
and the relatively large number of students who *didn't* instantly
recognize that it was the identical word list they "learned" earlier in
the school year.

When strategies are used to help students process information from lessons so it travels beyond temporary working memory
and into memory storage, they build the skills, confidence, and
competence that keep them engaged as lifelong learners of vocabulary, literature, and the world around them. Vocabulary lessons
and independent reading that activate multiple senses, relational
memories, and prior knowledge can connect the new information to multiple brain pathways to and from the memory storage
and retrieval areas. Successful brain research–based teaching builds
more connections and stronger circuits (Black, Isaacs, Anderson,
Alcantara, & Greenough, 1990). Students will have more roadways
to carry new information into their memory storage regions and
to carry out the stored knowledge when it is needed to identify
new words. Teaching neuro-*logical* strategies will result in vocabulary words becoming student-owned as these students continue to
achieve higher levels of reading, speaking, and writing.

6

Successful Reading Comprehension

The reading proficiency of adults in the United States has declined in the past decade to the point that only 31 percent of adults tested in 2003 could perform complex and challenging literacy activities (Kutner, Greenberg, Jin, Boyle, and Hsu, 2003).

With the current emphasis on phonics-heavy reading programs and decodable books aimed at practice and use of the phonics-heavy curricula, there is an associated delay in children's exposure to rich, meaningful, personally relevant, and enjoyable literature in the classroom. Many teachers enhance unstimulating decodables by reading aloud from engaging books to show children that learning to read is a worthwhile goal and written material can be wondrous and exciting.

After students do learn to understand the individual words they read in texts, new brain areas need stimulation and practice to recall the words long enough to understand complete sentences. The information from the beginning of a sentence or preceding sentences in a paragraph must be kept accessible while the next segment of text is read. Students also need practice storing and retrieving the content of sentences so that they can comprehend pages, chapters, and finally entire texts.

Reading difficulties can interfere at each step of the comprehension process. For example, to comprehend a story, the reader has to continually recall the preceding words, sentences, and pages in the story. For some students, the process of decoding consumes so much of the brain's metabolic activity that there appears to be an inadequate flow of oxygen and glucose to support the metabolism in the brain's cortical areas of memory storage. Without the ability to connect each new word, sentence, or page with those that came before, children cannot build a comprehensive understanding of the words they read (Long & Chong, 2001).

Goals of Reading Comprehension Strategies

Strategies to build comprehension are available to increase neural efficiency at each step of the comprehension process. Skilled readers comprehend more successfully than less skilled readers because skilled readers use strategies such as activating background knowledge to comprehend text and to draw valid inferences about what they have read (Dickson, Simmons, & Kame'enui, 1998). They also differ from unskilled readers in their ability to decode fluently and accurately (Perfetti & Bolger, 2004; Vellutino, Fletcher, Snowling, & Scanlon, 2004).

The neuroimaging and neurocognitive research about reading comprehension covers how the brain takes in new information through a variety of neural networks using patterns, categories, and relational connections, and builds the new data into comprehended knowledge. The strategies that influence the brain's metabolic neural activity in the regions involved in this processing of raw data into stored, comprehended knowledge will be described including engaged learning, personal connection, background knowledge, meaningful context, prediction, critical analysis, and metacognition.

As comprehension increases, so does appreciation of reading for both knowledge and pleasure. Constructing meaning from text or spoken language is not a separate literacy skill, but a merging of all acquired prior knowledge, personal experience, and vocabulary with the strategies of deductive and inductive reasoning and making connections. To be successful at reading comprehension, students need to actively process what they read. That processing skill requires that students have automatic reading skills and fluency, necessary vocabulary, and text-appropriate background knowledge. Successful comprehension is augmented when students have practice with strategies for monitoring their understanding, increasing their intrinsic interest in the text, and creating goals and purpose for their reading.

To comprehend text, the reader must be able to decode words or recognize words and access text integration processes to construct meaning and retain the content of the words long enough for it to stimulate their stores of related information in their long-term memories (Cunningham & Stanovich, 1998). Beginning comprehension instruction builds on children's linguistic and conceptual knowledge (Snow, Burns, & Griffin, 1998) and includes explicit instruction on strategies such as summarizing, predicting, and self-monitoring for understanding (Learning First Alliance, 1998). Additional comprehension skills that must be taught and practiced include assessing and connecting with students' background knowledge, preteaching of new vocabulary, clarification of key concepts, linking to prior knowledge and personal relevance, instruction in strategies, teacher-guided and student-centered discussions about the content, previewing, predicting, summarizing, selecting main ideas, self-monitoring, and teacher feedback for understanding (Snow, Burns, & Griffin, 1998).

The boy at the lighthouse would not have been willing to climb a single step if, at the very base of the staircase, he could see the hundreds of steps that awaited him. However, even at his most fatigued if he were coaxed to see if he could climb a single step, isolated from that daunting staircase, he would have tried and succeeded. The approach I use is to first guide students to *access* their individual comprehension competencies and then to help each student establish challenging but achievable reading comprehension goals.

Comprehension Motivators

Just as motivation and engagement are the keys to students persevering through any of the early reading skills that are frustrating, these also are the cornerstones of the strategies I use to connect students to reading comprehension skill acquisition. I plan strategies that resonate with the affective filters and dopamine-pleasure release to stimulate student motivation and engagement through connections and use texts that are relevant and therefore interesting to my students.

When I plan my preteaching or previews I keep in mind the goals of connecting to students' previous positive experiences, real-world applications, and personal interests as well as captivating their interest through novelty and imagination stimulation, helping them construct goals for their reading, and supporting them as they strive for realistic self-challenge. The previewing and motivating process begins with activating prior knowledge, building connections, establishing goals for reading with purpose, and preteaching information needed for successful comprehension of the particular text.

Activate Prior Knowledge

Prior knowledge activation starts with what I know about my students from observation, assessments, conversations, parent and student conferences, information from previous teachers, peer interviews, and interest inventories. I use this knowledge to select books and to help students relate a new book to their lives, interests, backgrounds, and prior knowledge.

Fluency practice helps students recognize words when they read them. Similarly, when students are prompted to recall prior stored knowledge they may stimulate related neural networks as they consciously look for links in their prior knowledge to events, people, and places in the story.

Strategies include

• Activate students' background knowledge through discussions about interesting topics that will be included in the book before they read it.

• Let students who already know something about the topic or author share their experiences and insights with classmates so these student experts feel engaged and their enthusiasm builds interest among their classmates.

• Continue to activate prior knowledge even after the book is started to sustain student goal-based and motivated reading. Every few chapters, use prereading sessions that include questions and prompts related to additional prior knowledge that becomes pertinent during these later parts of the book.

Big Picture First

Before reading a text that will offer an achievable comprehension challenge, all students, and especially global learners, benefit from some preview of the big picture. This can serve to prompt prior knowledge, stimulate personal interest, demonstrate real world value to the reading, and guide students to develop personal goals that will keep them connected to the content of what they read so the information will go from working memory to long-term memory.

Big picture exploration can start even before formal prediction or KWL activities by having discussions or activities related to the topic of the book. Guest speakers, videos, art projects, field trips, current event stories in newspapers, cross-curricular connections, and journal or quick-writing prompts about the topic can all build student engagement and motivation. These priming activities will hopefully start the stimulation of brain categories that will be pattern templates for students' brains to recognize, encode, and transport new information to connect with the stored patterns.

Prereading

Prereading prepares students for the content, focus, organization, and level of difficulty of challenging comprehension material. The goal of prereading is to give students an overview of the topic, book, or story to be read so they can develop mental templates upon which to pattern the new information. Prereading can include activities to build interest and attention, explore keywords, create connections and background knowledge, and establish reading goals.

Build Interest and Attention: Just as discrepant events can be powerful motivators for students to actively think during science lessons, they also work in reading. Ask questions about the book topic that piques their interest or offer tantalizing but brief descriptions of the theme or story organization. Reading a surprising or intriguing passage from the book can be the start of a discussion that allows students to give opinions as to what it might mean and in what context. This discrepant event builds insights they can use later in prediction activities.

Students are using frontal lobe executive function cognition when they look ahead, predict, anticipate, analyze, and evaluate, making adjustments as they read. Another advantage of observing how students respond to preview activities and information is discovering more about their learning styles. For example, if a child is successful at reading previewing, this strategy can be suggested for difficulties he is having in working through math problems. He can be shown how to use lecture or text cues to preview and predict what information is important to study for a test.

Explore Key Words: Pre-instruction in the vocabulary words that students need to stay comfortable and connected to the text has been discussed in the previous chapter. For textbooks in social studies, science, mathematics, or grammar, keywords are often found at the beginning of a chapter. In literature you may need to preselect keywords as you plan weekly vocabulary lists.

Build Connections and Background Knowledge: After giving students with prior knowledge opportunities to connect with their knowledge and using the big picture to engage others in the topic, more can be done to include the remaining students. To bring all students up to the level of background knowledge needed, consider the suggestion of Vygotsky (1978) that learning always proceeds from the known to the new. When teachers provide background knowledge before students read, story comprehension improves (Kinzer & Leu, 1997; Sharp et al., 1995). Prepared students have more equal footing. As you provide this background knowledge through cross-curricular thematic lessons, videos, and directed instruction, you can keep students engaged with open-ended discussions that help students make connections between the information and their own interests.

To bridge the gap between text and students, consider classroom activities that connect with the book they will read. If they will be reading about a leader of a colony during the colonial period in the future United States, a prereading discussion can start with making a class list of the qualities they would want in the leader of a colony they would select to join. Students could volunteer to be mock candidates using a set of platform policies about colony goals and governing. Classmates can have a debate about whom they support as a candidate or which platform appeals to them. As students start to read the book, they will have investment in seeing which characteristics and policies were supported in the book and how things turned out.

Establish Reading Goals: As with any unit of study, even after students see the big picture, it is motivating for them to know why the book is important enough to be worth their effort. In addition to the real world interests and connections they develop during big picture activities, consider how each student in the class can develop personally meaningful goals to keep him or her engaged and focused during the reading. When part of their goals include finding information to support their predictions or to answer their questions, students approach the reading with more motivation. Their goals can give them a purpose for reading, encourage them to monitor their comprehension, and stimulate active thinking as they read. It helps to make the correlation between the successes students had when they worked toward previous goals. It is motivating when students see their comprehension skill levels increase in response to their practice just as they recognized that success correlated with their practice in sports, musical instrument rehearsal, keyboarding, or learning multiplication tables.

Have students discuss goals of what they want from the book, both in terms of knowledge they want to acquire and comprehension skills they want to build. They can write down questions they want the text to answer and information they seek independently even before the formal KWL activity. For some students, goal-directed reading will occur automatically. For other students with limited comprehension, focus, or English language skills, you will need to check in with them for more formal discussions of goals. Possibly, you will work with them on their individual charting of goals, practice, and achievements as you continue to remind them of their previous successes with practice leading to proficiency in things they had an interest in mastering.

Predicting

One of the most popular and brain-compatible forms of predicting is the KWL chart. This strategy gives students opportunities to activate prior knowledge as they consider what they know about the subject (prior knowledge), what they would like to learn (goal), and later, what they comprehend and learned. KWL activities chart a course for student goal-directed reading that can motivate comprehension. Students not only want to acquire the information they seek, but they are personally invested in seeing if their predictions and those of their classmates on the list of "What I think I know" are correct.

To make this activity more personal, students can first work alone to create their own K and W parts of the chart. After class discussion and creation of a class KWL chart that can remain up throughout the reading of the book or story, students can add the element of personal engagement through choice by adding to their personal lists the K and W statements and questions posed by classmates that resonate with their own brains.

Another type of prediction to use before the class begins reading a new book or chapter is a nongraded true/false, multiple choice, or fill-in-the-blank prediction page. On this page, students respond based on their own opinions to questions that will be answered as they move along in the story. This strategy is designed to keep students' reticular activating systems and affective filters primed to seek out the information that will confirm or refute their predictions so they are motivated to follow the story through personal engagement.

Because students keep their own prediction pages, they can give themselves stars or make corrections in their responses as the story progresses and class discussions clarify the answers. When they predict correctly, this may encourage them to share their prediction reasoning with the class because they built confidence from their correct predictions. Although students are always encouraged to state or write reasons for their predictions, once the class discussion takes place following the unfolding of the plot, students can continue with the mental manipulation to build executive function and long-term memory by adding more data to the evidence they list in support of their prediction. By correcting incorrect predictions in their papers, students will have practiced writing the correct comprehension response and have that information to study when they need it to write a paper or take a test.

Extending Comprehension Strategies

Comprehension lessons can also achieve specific objectives beyond students' understanding of the meaning of the words they read or hear. The added goals can include cognitive manipulation of the information by actively processing it through executive function in higher cognitive activities such as

- Considering the information in another context
- Making interpretations
- Discovering new personal connections or connections to previous films or literature
- Using information acquired to modify their predictions
- Analyzing and comparing characters and interpreting their relationships and motives
- Inferring causes and effects
- Summarizing the plot
- Deducing the theme or author's message

As the lessons progress, consider listing which comprehension objectives you are working toward during the day's discussion or activity so students become consciously aware of how skilled readers interact with text to build comprehension, knowledge, and engagement. Students can be encouraged to refer to the class list that is developed as they participate in lessons with one or more of these goals of comprehension.

Comprehension Strategies Modified for Better Brain Fit

When I began to keep track of the strategies I use and how they might be modified to be compatible with my understanding of the ways the brain reads, I found it most useful to structure strategies for the specific comprehension goals I had for each book. I realized that my comprehension goals depended on the content of the book. Previously, I had followed a rather formulaic system of using almost the same strategies in the same sequence to help students summarize, describe, interpret, contrast, predict, associate, distinguish, or generalize. Now I use the strategies best suited to my goals for student comprehension.

Consider prioritizing your comprehension goals for each book you use and then select the strategies you find most pertinent to those goals. You can use these strategies in the order that seems best suited to the book you are working with.

Summarizing

Summarization connects reading and memory by linking understanding of text to remembering. This strategy makes sense as an introduction to incorporate before beginning the other strategies for several reasons, some not brain related. For example, students may not have done the reading homework, may have been absent for several days of class reading, or may have special needs that benefit from hearing summaries of what was read.

Students who are having trouble with summarizing can build up to story summarizing through scaffolded practice. Students can start with a summary of events such as weekend activities or sporting events. They can record their summaries and compare with classmates to see how accurate and *precise* they were.

As students practice summarizing text, remind them to refer to the text to support their opinions and inferences. They may realize they need to take notes to help them with summaries. If students have trouble with summarizing or recognizing the main idea in a paragraph or story, they can practice summarizing familiar stories from other books they read or stories they have heard multiple times. Summarizing movies or television shows can also scaffold text summarizing. Students can also practice finding the main idea of paragraphs or pages. A list of guiding questions can be provided to start them off such as, "Who is the subject of the paragraph?" and "What is the most important information or most important thing described in the page or paragraph?" Students may find it helpful to write margin or reading log notes while they read to summarize key points after reading longer passages.

Students can be given written prompts as questions to consider as they first summarize plot and then deduce theme. Questions they can first write responses to and later ask themselves as they read include

• Who is the main character and what important things has he or she done so far?

• What plot information relates to things the main character did?

• What qualities does the author seem to think are good or important in people?

• Has there been any conflict and resolution so far?

• What does this information suggest to you about the author's message, reason for writing the story, and therefore, the theme?

Summarizing can help students at all levels of comprehension when it precedes the class discussion about other parts of the text analysis. The class discussion can be orchestrated so students can contribute to summaries at their individual comprehension and language levels. I structure these summary discussions by selecting or encouraging volunteers whom I believe will describe the basic outlines before I call on students who I know will add depth to the summary.

Compare and Contrast

Comparing and contrasting helps students make associations between elements of story, character, setting, and theme. Student personal connection to comparison/contrast activities can include debates where students choose sides and support their selected character's point of view. Then they can switch roles and support the contrasting character's perspective. Students can discuss the similarities and differences between their lives and those of the characters.

Comparisons and contrasts are beneficial both within the context of the book and with reference to previous reading, stories, or real people. This activity is well suited for analytical learners and allows all students opportunities to manipulate information through executive function. Venn diagrams can be added to the compare-contrast activity.

I-dentify: Building Personal Relationships with Content

Comprehension is defined as "intentional thinking during which meaning is constructed through interactions between text and reader" (Harris & Hodges, 1995). Readers can derive meaning from text and build ownership of what they read and hear when they actively relate the ideas to their own knowledge and experiences and construct mental representations with personal connections as they read.

Make Inferences and Ask Questions

Making inferences can engage problem-solving thinking processes that build interest. Asking themselves questions as they read can add additional information for students to seek as they read with a purpose to find the answers. Other questions can become points of class discussion.

Self-Monitoring

Self-monitoring requires students to learn to stop periodically to take notes of the words they do not understand or parts of the plot that don't make sense. Students can use timers or signals from teachers to stop at periodic intervals or at appropriate breaks in chapters or subchapters to monitor their own conceptual understanding. Through instruction, modeling, and practice, students can also be taught to stop periodically to construct mental images and do independent summaries of their understanding of the action or character development every few pages. When students become more experienced, they can transition to making their own inferences, predictions, and mental notes as they to read.

When students have difficulty remembering to stop for this self-monitoring, I have had them use sticky notes every designated number of pages so they remember to stop and self-monitor. Depending on the comprehension strategy they are working on, they may also jot down the words that confused them, their inferences, or a few words of summary. These are not formal notes to be saved for reference, but rather prompts to use for the comprehension activity they are working on with the self-monitoring strategy.

Teacher Modeling of Comprehension Strategies

Teacher modeling of comprehension strategies helps students learn how to identify which strategies are most useful for different comprehension tasks and types of text. Although some strategies are acquired informally, explicit instruction in strategy application can make their use more clear and increase the likelihood that students will use them correctly and independently.

Some of the benefits of modeling may coincide with the research described in Chapter 1 regarding mirror neurons. Just as mirror neurons suggest that watching an action activates the same neurons as are activated when the subject performs the action, students may be building neural connections by observing the modeling of the comprehension-building technique.

When modeling the comprehension strategy, the goal is to make the strategy explicit. Speaking your thinking aloud while also writing steps down offers the information to students through two sensory inputs. When you stop before demonstrating sequential parts of a multistep strategy you can make comments such as

- "I'm using self-monitoring now to see if I understand why this character did something that doesn't make sense to me. I thought he was going to help his friend, but the note he wrote to the teacher seems to be something that would get his friend in trouble. I wonder if I missed something about the story or about this character's motives. I will go back to the part where he talks with his friend and see if I can clarify my comprehension."

• "I think I need to make a timeline because the author seems to switch between past, present, and future."

• "I don't know the word 'hearth,' but it sounds like something in the house that is warm, maybe a fire pit or a cooking place. I'll read the sentence again with the word 'fireplace' instead of hearth and see if it makes sense."

Students may benefit from seeing the use of the strategy with material with which they are already familiar so they are comfortable and are successful with the strategy the first time they practice with it. They can then do teacher-guided whole-class activities using the strategy related to the class text. During the modeling transition stage, you can do the activity with volunteer student models who have practiced their presentation with you first. Through repetitions of the task, students take on more and more of the responsibility, and the reason for the strategy is reviewed several times.

The next step is for students to practice in pairs and independently on material especially for them from the text. Frequent monitoring of student practice with feedback continues to ensure that all students are practicing the strategy correctly. Independent work can continue, but at the conclusion all students record the strategy and their impression about how it worked for them and when they might use it again. This becomes part of a continuing personal strategy list that is added to during metacognition activities and becomes a resource for future independent reading comprehension.

Graphic or Visual Organizers

Graphic or visual organizers include maps, webs, graphs, charts, frames, and clusters. Visual displays can increase comprehension, organization, summarizing, prioritizing, memorization, and analysis by helping students construct and visualize relationships. Graphic organizers are compatible with the brain's process of patterning information for recognition, transportation along neural networks, and storage in categories. There are visual organizers that coincide with most of the previously described strategies for facilitating comprehension and memory. As younger readers develop the skill of predicting or previewing by looking at parts of the book, graphic organizers can help them chart the relationship between headings, subheadings, and chapters. Deducing the main idea from supporting evidence for plot or character comprehension can be visually contextualized with graphic organizers. These visual organizers help students recognize the patterns of subplots and family relationships as they translate text into visual displays.

Examples of Graphic Organizers

• **Venn diagrams** can be used to compare or contrast information from two books such as two by the same author or about similar topics. Venn diagrams can compare two or more parts of a book such as characters or settings.

• **Timelines** can order events within a text in the sequence in which they occur. Students can practice by making timelines for their favorite activities or of other things they do in sequence such as making a sandwich, dressing for team sports, or turning on the computer and logging on to their level of play on a computer game. They can also make timelines of their lives from birth to current age with branches for important events.

- **Story webs** can be written on a graphic organizer with questions based on "Want to Know" or predictions after previewing but before reading the book. The web adds to students' goal-directed connection to reading and focuses comprehension. Branches or spokes around the book title can include the questions they posed during the KWL or other prediction activity such as: What does the title have to do with the book (or story)? Where and when does the setting include the places on the map of Middle Earth in the front of the book? What evidence is there that this book is historical fiction? Who are the main characters? Why is there a picture of a boat on the cover? Why is there an illustration of a sad boy? Why is he sad? Encourage students to look for the answers to the questions as they read the story. When individual students find answers they can add them to their webs and at the end of the reading session share them with the class and be encouraged to give reasons for their answers. Students can add ideas they agree with on the class list to their own lists. These can become ways to review the story before subsequent reading sessions or before the test or writing assignment.

Free Web sites offer downloadable templates for visual/graphic organizers—such as http://www.edhelper.com/teachers/graphic_organizers.htm—or you can purchase computer software programs such as *Inspiration,* Kidspiration for K–5 students (http://www.inspiration.com/productinfo/kidspiration/index.cfm), or SmartDraw (http://www.smartdraw.com).

After Modeling

Assisting and instructing students to do complex cognitive tasks such as guiding them through these strategies in actual, concrete activities engages them in purposeful, carefully scaffolded learning processes focused on challenging learning tasks in their zone of proximal development (ZPD), the cognitive region just beyond what the student can accomplish alone. With enough assisted practice, the strategy then becomes part of the student's internalized reading comprehension repertoire and enters his zone of actual development (ZAD)—what he can do alone and unassisted. Practice occurs through reciprocal reading or partner or pair reading comprehension activities.

Reciprocal Reading for Comprehension

Reciprocal reading allows students to work in their ZPDs without anxiety. After the teacher models the strategy and reminds students about the importance of mutual support and encouragement, students have the opportunity to take the role of leader in this small group activity. After someone reads a portion of text aloud as the group follows along, volunteers give oral summaries, and the leader encourages other group members to add information. Depending on what strategy is being practiced, the leader then encourages the group members to suggest possible predictions, draw comparisons, make inferences, describe personal connections to text, or pose questions to consider as goals for the next reading section.

Peer Teaching

Assessing students' understanding by asking if they have any questions is often inadequate. Sometimes students think they understand when they do not actually understand. Other students may have questions but feel too much anxiety to ask questions in whole-class or even small groups. Peer work can provide a lower stress opportunity for students to share their understanding. For a partner who has a clear comprehension, teaching the information to a classmate reinforces the knowledge by reactivating the neural circuits where the knowledge is stored. The verbal communication of knowledge requires more structured thinking and gives the student another opportunity to process the knowledge in executive function to reach an even higher level of understanding. Peer work in comprehension is preceded with modeling and practice in active listening such that students share their own ideas only after paraphrasing the ideas expressed by their partner. When peers are well paired and practice active listening, the level of challenge, support, and meaningful feedback can be individualized for achievable challenge so students experience accomplishment without frustration.

Lists of comprehension questions suited to the book and strategy being practiced can be given to the pairs to guide their discussions. The other partner can also explain vocabulary words that may have been confusing to one partner.

The partner-share will give more students confidence to join in the subsequent class discussion. Even for those who don't feel ready, the partner-share will be a review and that added engagement with the previously confusing material will help them get more connected as active listeners to the ensuing class discussion. After partner-sharing, students can work together to add more information to their ongoing graphic organizers.

Independent Activities

Independent comprehension activities such as papers, projects, or original graphic organizers can give students opportunities to demonstrate their comprehension and their improvement. This is also the time for students to chart their individual comprehension goal progress or write in their literature response logs so they can experience the dopamine-pleasure response to recognizing their growing skills and feel encouraged to persevere.

Literature Log

Literature logs are personal journals where students respond to the book. Initially, I provide prompts, but when students become more independent they are encouraged to respond to parts of a book they select as personally significant or interesting. Student response to some literature may be very personal, so I offer students options to keep sections private. One approach is to permit students to fold over and tape the private pages so you can see the amount they wrote but still respect the privacy of their reflections.

Consider using literature logs to pull students in through their comfort and interest zones thus lowering their affective filters so new information can penetrate their amygdalas, connect with personal and relational memories, and be consolidated and stored as long-term memory. In their logs, students are prompted to include quotes, paraphrase conversations, and briefly summarize parts of the plot that cause them to pause and think. Asking students to select the sections that are most meaningful to them supports student comfort and resonance. Prompts to encourage personal connections include the following suggestions:

• Which character reminds you of someone you have met or something about yourself?

• Write about a time when you faced a problem similar to one confronted by a character in this book. How did you react? Did reading this book give you any ideas about what you might have done differently in your own experience?

• Describe a situation when you have been surprised, frustrated, frightened, angry, sad, or confused like the character in the book.

Note Taking for Comprehension

Modeling

As with most activities where new strategies are employed, consider modeling the strategy of selecting what text information is important enough to warrant note taking. When the class is of the right age and responsiveness level, I've worn a baseball cap as I model places where I would take notes. I read the text aloud and project it on an overhead or from a computer onto a television monitor. When I come to a phrase or section that I think is fairly important for students to include in their notes or that it is critical to the theme, plot, or characterization of the story, I turn the cap sideways and say a few words about why I am noting this section of text. When I read a passage that has very important, noteworthy information, I completely reverse the cap and do my think-aloud. After this type of modeling, I may select appropriately skilled student volunteers to read the next passage in front of the class. To support the volunteers, I may stand in the back of the room and rotate the cap to prompt them when they come to text that should be included in notes. The student can then write the notes as she sees fit on the overhead projector, and I invite classmates to add note points.

After adequate modeling, I have let the students try note taking in pairs as they reread text we have already read and discussed. This can be part of the paired-reading or peer-teaching activity. After the pairs finish, volunteers share lines from their notes as classmates add to their own notes the information they did not include initially that I confirm as noteworthy.

Question Making as Note Taking

Students can build on their goal-directed reading by adding questions they seek answers to as part of their daily notes.

Key Word Notes

Students who are overwhelmed by writing summaries about reading can start building the note-taking strategy by simply listing three or four key points or copying several sentences they feel are keys that unlock the meaning of what they just read. They can then add to their notes with information from classmates' notes I have copied (with permission) for students who need this support.

Note-Taking and Note-Making Strategy

To increase personal connections and relational memories, students can respond to the comprehension notes they take. (Strategy modified from one described by Schmeck, 1988.) Steps for this strategy: (1) Draw a line down the length of the paper about one-third of the way in. (2) Write notes about the text on the left side. (3) Make notes on right side with questions, comments, similarities, and personal connections.

Some student responses to literature logs and note taking include

- "I pay more attention to what I read when I take notes."
- "Because I have to decide what is important enough to write down I am actually thinking about the information and that helps me remember it better and follow the story more easily the next time we read."
- "Before I write it down I usually try to understand what it means. Sometimes when I don't understand, the note taking makes me look up words I don't understand or reread confusing parts."
- "After I take notes I am able to know more for class discussions."
- "If my notes are good, it saves me from having to reread the whole chapter before a test."

What this list of student note-taking benefits reflects is the brain processing I interpret as taking place when students' brains actively respond to the information they read. My goal is for students to exercise and develop their highest frontal lobe executive functions. When students summarize data as notes, they are making judgments and engaging in critical analyses when they effectively delete or merge information. My goal is for them to make connections and develop skills of relational memory making and patterning.

Memory and Comprehension

Working Memory

Active working memory is used when students retain the information from the beginning of a paragraph or chapter while reading the last sentences. Working memory is what lets students keep track of the beginning when they are trying to read and comprehend the end. Working memory keeps information in the conscious mind for about 20 seconds. New information, or just the passage of time, moves information out of working memory unless it is processed by active manipulation or patterned into connections with prior knowledge and existing stored categories of information such that the working memory becomes long-term memory.

Memory is also classified as implicit or explicit, with distinctive neural pathways seen on fMRI scans. Explicit memory includes memory of people, objects, places, facts, and events. These are processed as short-term memories in the prefrontal cortex. If they are manipulated through executive function and built into relational and long-term memories in the hippocampus, explicit memories are then stored in the parts of the cerebral cortex that correspond to the sense that first received the sensory input. (For example, auditory input that becomes long-term memory is stored in the auditory cortex of the temporal lobe, adjacent to the sensory intake area for response to sound.) Implicit memories are of skills, habits, and conditioning, and do not appear to be processed in the hippocampus, but rather in the cerebellum, striatum, and amygdala (Kandel, 2006).

Functional MRI studies have investigated the hypothesis that comprehension requires the reader to remember what has been read so it can be connected to new information and integrated with prior knowledge as the reading of a story continues (Long & Chong, 2001). Strategies I use are designed to build memory storage and retrieval skills to enhance reading comprehension.

Goals for Strategy Use in Building Memory for Comprehension

- Build patterned links to prior knowledge.
- Increase flow of comprehension information through the amygdala by lowering the affective filter with low-stress and high-interest activities so the information has a more efficient pathway

GRAY MATTER

An fMRI study scanned subjects predetermined to have low or high working memory on cognitive testing while they read sentences with ambiguous syntax. Participants read sentences with either a short or long region of temporary syntactic ambiguity while being scanned. The perisylvian region of the left temporal lobe and Broca's area in the left frontal lobe were identified as most active when subjects processed the syntactically ambiguous portion of the sentences. These same brain regions had previously been found to demonstrate high neural activity during working memory processing. The researchers believed that the activation of these same brain regions during specific tests for both working memory and syntactic analysis suggest that there could be a correlation between these two functions such that strategies that are structured to improve working memory span could benefit reading comprehension, especially of syntactically complex text (Friederici, Vos, & Friederici, 2004). I have incorporated interpretations from this and similar studies in strategies I use to strengthen students' comprehension of complex text such as highlighting, note taking, and summarizing strategies.

through the amygdala to the MTL (medial temporal lobe) and the higher cognitive functioning regions of the prefrontal cortex.

• Increase consolidation of information into students' long-term memories without the negative influence of high circulating cortisol to interfere with the storage and retrieval of this information needed for reading fluency (McGaugh, McIntyre, & Power, 2002).

• Highlighting, note taking, review, and rereading can restimulate newly formed patterns recently consolidated in the MTL and strengthen the long-term memory circuits in the neocortex.

Memory Building Activities

Reading Comprehension Quiz Show

The Reading Comprehension Quiz Show game involves as many teams as there are small reading groups. For younger children, the groups are monitored (by aide, teacher, parent assistant). Older students can be more independent, with adults as circulating observers. After a predetermined amount of text read-around by the small group (from a page to a chapter depending on length and student ability), all students write a question and answer on a note card. The question is about something in the text just read and will be used later in the contest when groups compete to answer questions about the whole book.

I start with the modeling and student practice of creating good questions after a whole-class reading of a page. I read a variety of what I consider good and poor questions and have students discuss why some questions might be too specific or too vague. I then have them suggest questions of their own and receive group feedback on these.

Before students do the question-making activity in their small reading groups, they practice or are reminded how to also give positive feedback as group members take turns reading their questions and answers aloud. Instead of the group deciding a question is not good enough to be used or that the answer is incorrect, they practice working together to improve the question so its originator has the satisfaction of having contributed a good question to the final contest.

At the time of the contest (which can be held several times over the course of a book that takes the class several weeks to read instead of just at the book's conclusion), I select the most reasonable comprehension review questions with the explanation that I took parts or ideas from each group member's questions to create the final ones I constructed.

Mnemonics

Mnemonics use the pattern-seeking brain action that looks for associations between the information it is receiving and the information that is already stored. If the brain can find a link to a pattern or existing category, the new information is more compatible with storage in long-term memory. Especially at the beginning of a book, where a number of locations, characters, and subplots are introduced without inherent meaning, students can practice creating mnemonics as organizational frameworks on which to hook new information.

One useful strategy is to list the names of the characters on a chart that can remain up during the reading of the book. Students can suggest character traits that are presented early in the book and that start with the same letter as the first letter of each character's name. A mnemonic can be created with the names and traits, such as: "Sarcastic Sally told timid Tina that brave Brian is looking for dishonest Dave."

Mnemonic acronyms can be used to aid comprehension of places where the action takes place in sequence. After making a timeline putting the settings in sequence, the first letter of a memorable word describing each setting can be written next to the setting. A real or nonsense word can be constructed from these first letters as is done in the mnemonic Roy G. Biv for the colors of the rainbow or PEMDAS for the order of operations in math computations (parentheses, exponents, multiplication, division, addition, subtraction). For the locations woods, attic, lake, tree, east gate, and road, my students created the mnemonic WALTER.

MOVES is a mnemonic acronym I created for my students to use when they review reading material for comprehension assessments. Each letter reminds them of another way to review the information through alternative sensory processing systems to stimulate multiple neural networks and strengthen long-term memory.

M: move/manipulate. Move around and use a physical action to remind you of a character's traits or a setting. Alternatively, manipulate models, dolls, or stuffed animals to act out important plot information.

O: organize. Create graphic organizers such as timelines and character charts to review important details.

V: visualize. Visualize characters, settings, and plot progressions in your mind so you'll have a visual network to link to when you want to retrieve text information.

E: enter. Enter the information you want to remember by typing it into a computer or writing it by hand. This combines tactile and visual memory.

S: say. Read the material aloud. Reading your notes or important passages aloud adds auditory memory to your networks of comprehension.

Demystifying Text

Whatever reading level students are at, there will always be some text that is challenging. A strategy that will help them reach their highest independent reading comprehension levels is not one of simplifying the text, but of demystifying it. When students learn to deconstruct text and see that even the most complex text is composed of simpler elements, the task of comprehension becomes less daunting.

Note Taking and Highlighting

As described earlier, note taking helps students keep track of what they read so they can reinforce the memory and also refresh their memory before beginning the next reading section (or when preparing for written response to literature or tests). Highlighting is a common technique, especially in course work with factual information such as history and science.

Modifying a strategy developed by professor Sheridan Blau of the University of California, Santa Barbara, I have students use colored markers to increase comprehension of complex text. Blau demonstrates the strategy with a poem and the instructions that students read the poem three times. Each time, students are instructed to underline anything they don't understand. The first underlining is in yellow, next in light blue, and third in green. (A modification without markers is to underline first in dotted lines, second in dashes, and last in uninterrupted lines.) Blau suggests that strong readers think about what they don't know and pay more attention to what is worth thinking about (Blau, 2003).

During the process, students understand more of the poem each time they read it. The process of underlining appears to focus attention on the phrases students initially underline because they are especially confusing. When students return to these lines, they are obliged to focus on them, and that activity appears to help them build comprehension skills such as concentration, persistence, and courage in the face of intellectual difficulties (Willis, 2005).

Lesson Consideration: For this strategy it is ideal if students own their own copies of the book so they can do the highlighting in the text. Even if funds don't permit purchase of books for students who would benefit from being able to place marks in their books, there are often books that have been removed from class circulation because the cover is damaged or they have water damage. Several such damaged books could be separated into sections such that the salvageable sections become available for students who need them. I have also made copies of difficult portions of the books for students to use for this highlighting strategy practice.

In some cases, when particular students need more scaffolding, the activity can be done as partner work with a classmate. For more challenged students, the highlighting can be done in advance by a parent, aide, or teacher.

I start early in the year making copies on overhead paper, placing a clear overhead projector paper over the copy and modeling the three-color marker process myself before doing it as a whole class with volunteers. I next have students work individually and share with partners or small groups using poems. After they develop confidence and begin to trust and enjoy the process, we move on to complicated passages from primary source history books and then to literature above their independent reading levels and individualized for the student's ability. The strategy even works with conceptual parts of science texts.

When I have used this strategy, some students have found it so useful they ask me to photocopy pages from their textbook reading homework that they did not understand during independent reading. This would be quite time consuming if it was needed for all students' reading all year. But as one would expect, as students become adept at the process, they are also developing their higher levels of comprehension, thinking, abstraction, and conceptualization. They discover that they can achieve the same degree of understanding by focused rereading. The end result is that they learn the material they need for those standardized tests, but because it is not processed through superficial rote memory, but rather relational and conceptual thinking using higher-level executive function skills, the learned material becomes part of their long-term memory available for retrieval and subsequent critical thinking connections far beyond test day.

I have seen the work these students have produced years after they leave my class, and I believe that Blau's strategy and a set of highlighters brightened their comprehension processing. I have found this process helpful with students at all reading comprehension levels. Students appear to develop their focus, patience, and reading frustration tolerance because the process itself is enjoyable (colored markers) and the success is immediately evident (less underlining each time because with rereading more is understood).

When Oberlin College class dean and study skills and reading instructor Melissa Ballard used this strategy in her Effective

Reading Strategies course with an Emily Dickinson poem, she wrote to me about significant improvement in every student's written responses and in the quality of whole-class discussions of the poem. She reported that her students seemed much more confident and even discussed how they might apply this strategy in classes as diverse as economics, Chinese, and biology.

In Ballard's class, students began by talking about the feelings they bring to the reading task, and some students were forthcoming about being "bad" at poetry or literary analysis, especially 19th century writing. One young man who had made that admission earlier in the year ended up being a major participant in the Dickenson discussion after using the highlighting strategy. When Ballard asked him if this seemed inconsistent, he said, "Maybe I've been underestimating myself."

Metacognition for Comprehension

Metacognition is thinking about thinking. Metacognitive strategies can be taught to help students mentally process the information they read and to recognize what they can do to build future success. Metacognition can be used when students first preview the book, to clarify their purpose for reading, and to set reading goals. As students read, metacognition strategies can help them recognize what they do or do not understand. Comprehension metacognition practice can be prompted by directing, modeling, scaffolding, and practicing to help students identify what they do not understand and select the best individual strategies to resolve their comprehension difficulties.

Instructions to Prompt Student Metacognition

• Stop periodically and consider if you understand what you just read. Try to summarize the information.

• Check what you are reading against what you already know.

• Make predictions about what is to come, and continually construct and revise a sense of the whole out of the parts.

• Identify the comprehension problem—is it a confusing vocabulary word, difficulty recalling past information about a character named in the passage, confusion about what happened previously that connects with the current action?

• Consider the strategies you have used before: look up the vocabulary word, check your graphic organizer or timeline, look back through the text, look ahead to see if the information in the next page will clarify your confusion. After repeated experience with their metacognitive strategies, students become more comfortable moving among the different strategies for different purposes.

• Metacognition is reinforced if after using a successful strategy students write a brief note on a list they keep of strategies that will serve them well in the future. These can be shared with classmates in whole-class discussions and added to class strategy lists.

Conclusion

....

After evaluating the advances in reading research through use of neuroimaging, neurotransmitter measurement, and neuroelectrical recordings that catch the brain in the act of reading, I am inspired to see how powerful the research becomes when educators apply the increasing understanding of the brain to develop and enhance their brain research-compatible reading instruction strategies.

I concur with my former fellow neurology resident Dr. John Mazziotta, now Neurology Department Chairman at UCLA, who contends that brain research already has and will continue to provide brain-based strategies and curriculum based on what the brain is wanting to do and can do best to the point that, "We might someday even use brain mapping to get to the bottom of the phonics versus whole language debate by scanning children who are just about to learn to read and using the scans and a battery of tasks to elucidate the strategy that each individual is using" (Mazziotta et al., 2001).

Mazziotta's work with the International Consortium for Brain Mapping (ICBM) led him to postulate that the human brain map will reveal the brain mechanisms involved in reading, memory, and learning and that this brain mapping could not only clarify the brain mechanisms that underlie learning, but help define strategies for better learning.

The emergence of the neuroscience of learning through neuroimaging during the reading processes provides valuable insights into how the brain learns to read, becomes a more successful reading organ, and how it responds to specific instructional strategies. The more we understand the brain processes of reading, the more successfully we will be able to develop and use the most suitable strategies to strengthen students' reading skills and their motivation to become lifelong readers and learners.

We are fortunate to be educators during this time of illuminating brain research devoted to reading. However, we are also educators in an era of increased standardization of testing used as a prominent measure of student, teacher, and school success. The resulting standardization of some reading curriculum is a contradiction to serving students' unique needs and reading aptitudes.

I hope I have been able to provide you with information to help you meet your challenge and embrace your opportunity to incorporate the reading instruction strategies supported by interpretations of what I believe to be the most valid scientific discoveries and increasingly confirmed by cognitive testing and successful classroom implementation. The goal of reading instruction should be to help students achieve reading competency beyond test taking and rote memory skills. With continued collaboration among educators, cognitive psychologists, and neuroscientists, we can strive to help all students develop their reading skills so they can access the rich world of written information and imagination that is available in books, newspapers, magazines, online reading, and even on boxes of cereal.

Glossary

Alphabetic principle: Letters in written form represent sounds in spoken words.

Amygdala: A structure in the forebrain. It is part of the limbic system and plays a major role in emotional memory and the response to threat.

Autonomic nervous system: The ANS is that part of the nervous system responsible for regulating the activity of the body's other organs (e.g., skin, muscle, circulatory, digestive, endocrine).

Axon: The tiny fibrous extension of the neuron away from the cell body to other target cells (neurons, muscles, glands).

Broca's area: The brain center associated with the expressive and syntactic aspects of language.

Central nervous system: The portion of the nervous system comprised of the spinal cord and brain.

Cerebellum: This is a large cauliflower-looking structure on the top of the brain stem. This structure is very important in motor movement and motor-vestibular memory and learning.

Cerebral cortex: The outer layer of the cerebral hemispheres of the brain. The cortex mediates all conscious activity including planning, problem solving, language, and speech. It is also involved in perception and voluntary motor activity.

Choral reading: Students read text aloud together.

Cognition: The mental process by which we become aware of the world and use that information to problem solve and make sense out of the world. It is somewhat oversimplified, but cognition refers to thinking and all of the mental processes related to thinking.

Concepts of print: The rules or conventions of written language such as direction of reading sentences or reading of a book.

Decoding: The use of letter-sound relationships to connect printed words into spoken language.

Explicit thinking: Thinking where information is acquired directly from literal information or text without requiring the making of inferences or deductions.

Glia: Specialized cells that nourish, support, and complement the activity of neurons in the brain. Astrocytes are the most common and appear to play a key role in regulating the amount of neurotransmitter in the synapse by taking up excess neurotransmitter.

Hippocampus: This is a thin structure in the subcortex shaped like a seahorse. It is an important part of the limbic systems and plays a major role in learning, memory consolidation, and emotional regulation.

Homeostasis: The tendency of a physiological system (i.e., a neuron, neural system, or the body as a whole) to maintain its internal environment in a stable equilibrium.

Hypothalamus: This is a group of important nuclei that mediate many important functions. It is located at the base of the brain and connected to the pituitary by a network of specialized blood vessels. The hypothalamic nuclei are involved in regulating many of the body's internal organs via hormonal communication. The hypothalamus is a key part of the hypothalamic-pituitary-adrenal (HPA) axis that is so important in the stress response.

Imitation learning: Mimicry learning through the activation of mirror neurons.

Implicit thinking: Requires the student to use prior knowledge to deduce an answer.

Input hypothesis (IH): Supported by Krashen, this theory contends that language is learned by understanding messages that are communicated particularly through comprehensible input (language that is at or slightly above the language level that a person can understand).

Limbic system: A group of functionally and developmentally linked structures in the brain (including the amygdala, cingulate cortex, hippocampus, septum, and basal ganglia). The limbic system is involved in regulation of emotion, memory, and processing complex socio-emotional communication.

Mirror neurons: Mirror neurons fire both when an animal performs an action and when the animal observes the same action performed by another animal. These neurons "mirror" the behavior of another animal, as though the observer was performing the action.

Neuron: A cell specialized for receiving and transmitting information. While neurons have tremendous heterogeneity in structure, they all have some form of dendritic projections that receive incoming information and axonal projections that communicate to other cells.

Neurotransmitter: A chemical that is released from a neuron that can relay information to another cell by binding to a receptor on the membrane of the target cell.

Oligodendrocytes: The glia that specialize to form the myelin sheath around many axonal projections.

Patterning: The brain process of structuring information received through the senses (sensory data input) into the format or coding by which information travels from brain cell to brain cell. In response to sensory input our brains build new connections and stimulate existing neural networks by detecting patterns and evaluating new stimuli for clues that will help us connect incoming information with stored patterns, existing categories of data, or past experiences.

Phonemic awareness: The perception of the differences between sounds in spoken words and ability to manipulate the smallest units of sound in spoken thought processes such as blending, segmenting, and adding phonemes.

Phonological recoding (phonological naming): This corresponds with a distinctly different bilateral network, including the right posterior superior temporal gyrus, right middle temporal gyrus, and left ventral inferior frontal gyrus. These areas do not overlap with the regions for phonological awareness or phonetic recording.

Phonologic processing: Identifying the individual sounds that make up words (phonemes) and subsequently identifying the words that the sounds combine to make.

Plasticity: This refers to the remarkable capacity of the brain to change its molecular, microarchitectural, and functional organization in response to injury or experience.

Quantitative EEG (qEEG): This measures the changes in the brain's electrical activity (brain wave responses) when individual brain areas are stimulated in sequence along a neural pathway.

Synapse: This is the specialized space between two neurons that is involved in information transfer. A neurotransmitter is released from one neuron, enters the synaptic cleft (space), and sends a signal to the post-synaptic neuron by occupying its receptors.

Thalamus: This is a paired structure of two tiny egg-shaped structures in the diencephalon. This structure is a crucial area for integrating and organizing sensory information that comes into the brain. In the thalamus, this information is processed and forwarded to the key cortical areas where more processing and integrating will take place.

Wernicke's area: A region of the posterior section of the left superior temporal gyrus cortex active in understanding and producing comprehensible language.

Zone of actual development (ZAD): What students can do alone and unassisted.

Zone of proximal development (ZPD): The difference between what a child can do with help and what he or she can do without guidance.

References

Anderson, R. C. (1999). Research foundations to support wide reading. In *Reading research anthology: The why of reading instruction.* Novato, CA: Arena Press. 14–21.

Aron, A., Gluck, M., & Poldrack, R. (2006). Long-term test-retest reliability of fMRI in classification learning task. *NeuroImage, 29*(3), 1000–1006.

Aron, R., Shohamy, D., Clark, J., Myers, C., Gluck, M., & Poldrack, R. (2004). Human midbrain sensitivity to cognitive feedback and uncertainty during classification learning. *Journal of Neurophysiology, 92*(2), 1144–1152.

Baker, S., Simmons, D. C., & Kame'enui, E. J. (1997). Vocabulary acquisition: Research bases. In D. C. Simmons & E. J. Kame'enui (Eds.), *What reading research tells us about children with diverse learning needs: Bases and basics,* pp. 183–217. Mahwah, NJ: Erlbaum.

Beck, I., & McKeown, M. (1991). Social studies texts are hard to understand: Mediating some of the difficulties. *Language Arts, 68*(6), 482–490.

Beck, I., & McKeown, M. (2003). Taking delight in words: Using oral language to build young children's vocabularies. *American Educator, 27*(1), 36–46.

Beeman, M., & Chiarello, C. (1998). Complementary right- and left-hemisphere language comprehension. *Current Directions in Psychology Science, 7*(1), 2–7.

Biemiller, A. (2001). Teaching vocabulary: Early, direct, and sequential. *American Educator, 25*(47), 24–28.

Biemiller, A. (2004). Teaching vocabulary in the primary grades: Vocabulary instruction needed. In J. F. Baumann & E. J. Kame'enui (Eds.), *Reading vocabulary: Research to practice* (pp. 89–94). New York: Guilford Press.

Black, J., Isaacs, K., Anderson, B., Alcantara, A., & Greenough, W. (1990). Learning causes synaptogenesis in cerebral cortex. *Proceedings of the National Academy of Science, 87,* 5568–5572.

Black, K., Hershey, T., Koller, J., Videen, T., Mintun, M., Price, J., Perlmutter, J. (2002). A possible substrate for dopamine-related changes in mood and behavior: Prefrontal and limbic effects of a D3-preferring dopamine agonist. *Proceedings of the National Academy of Science, 99*(26), 17113-17118.

Blau, S. (2003). *The literature workshop: Teaching texts and their readers.* Portsmouth, NH: Heinemann.

Brooks, R., & Meltzoff, N. (2005). The development of gaze following and its relation to language. *Developmental Science, 8*(6), 535–543.

Buccino, G., Lui, F., Canessa, N., Patteri, I., Lagravinese, G., Benuzzi, F., Porro, C., & Rizzolatti, G. (2004). Neural circuits involved in the recognition of actions performed by nonconspecifics: An fMRI study. *Journal of Cognitive Neuroscience, 16*(1), 114–126.

Chall, J. S., Jacobs, V. A., & Baldwin, L. E. (1990). *The reading crisis: Why poor children fall behind.* Cambridge, MA: Harvard University Press.

Chugani, H. (1996). Neuroimaging of developmental nonlinearity and developmental pathologies. In R. W. Thatcher et al. (Eds), *Developmental neuroimaging,* (pp. 187–195). San Diego, CA: Academic Press.

Chugani, H. (1998). Biological basis of emotions: Brain systems and brain development. *Pediatrics, 102,* 1225–1229.

Chugani, H., Phelps, M. E., & Mazziotta, J. C. (1987). Positron emission tomography study of human brain function development. *Annals of Neurology, 22,* 487–497.

Coles, G. (2004). Danger in the classroom: 'Brain glitch' research and learning to read. *Phi Delta Kappan, 85*(5), 344–351.

Coward, A. (1990). *Pattern thinking.* New York: Praeger.

Cunningham, A. E., & Stanovich, K. E. (1997). Early reading acquisition and its relation to reading experience and ability 10 years later. *Developmental Psychology, 33,* 934–945.

Cunningham, A., & Stanovich, K. (1998, Spring/Summer). What reading does for the mind. *The American Educator, 22,* 8–15.

Devlin, T., Matthews, P., & Rushworth, M. (2003). Semantic processing in the left inferior prefrontal cortex: A combined fMRI and transcranial magnetic stimulation study. *Journal of Cognitive Neuroscience, 15,* 79–83.

Dickson, S., Simmons, D., & Kame'enui, E. (1998). Text organization: Research bases. In D. C. Simmons & E. J. Kame'enui (Eds.), *What reading research tells us about children with diverse learning needs* (pp. 239–278). Mahwah, NJ: Erlbaum.

Drew, D. (1996). *Aptitude revisited: Rethinking math and science education for America's next century.* Baltimore: Johns Hopkins University Press.

Eldridge, L. L. , Engel, S. A., Zeineh, M. M., Bookheimer, S. Y., & Knowlton, B. J. (2005). A dissociation of encoding and retrieval processes in the human hippocampus. *Journal of Neuroscience, 25,* 3280–3286.

Epstein, H. T. (1978). Growth spurts during brain development: Implications for educational policy and practice. In J. S. Chall & A. F. Mirsky (Eds.), *Education and the brain* (pp. 343–370). Chicago: University of Chicago Press.

Fiebach, C., Vos, S., & Friederici, A. (2004). Neural correlates of syntactic ambiguity in sentence comprehension for low and high span readers. *Journal of Cognitive Neuroscience, 16*(9), 1562–1575.

Fielding–Barnsley, R. (1997). Explicit instruction in decoding benefits children high in phonemic awareness and alphabet knowledge. *Scientific Studies of Reading, 1*(1), 85–98.

Foorman, B. (1995). Research on "The Great Debate": Code-oriented versus whole language approaches to reading instruction. *School Psychology Review, 24*(3), 376–392.

Friederici, C., Vos, S., & Friederici, A. (2004). Neural correlates of syntactic ambiguity in sentence comprehension for low and high span readers. *Journal of Cognitive Neuroscience, 16,* 1562–1575.

Gabrieli, J., & Preston, A. (2003). Working smarter, not harder. *Neuron, 37*(2), 191–192.

Gardner, H. (1983). *Frames of mind: The theory of multiple intelligences.* New York: Basic Books.

Gardner, H. (1999). *Intelligence reframed: Multiple intelligences for the 21st century.* New York: Basic Books.

Geake, J., (2006). How the brain learns to read. *Journal of Research in Reading, 29*(1), 135.

Gorman, M. (2000). *Human values in a technological age.* Keynote speech delivered at the LITA National Forum, November 2–5, 2000, in Portland, OR. Available: http://www.ala.org/ala/lita/litapublications/ital/vol20/number1/gorman.htm.

Grabowski, T. J., Damasio, H., & Damasio, A. R. (1998). Premotor and prefrontal correlates of category-related lexical retrieval. *NeuroImage, 7*(3), 232–243.

Greenlee–Moore, M. E., & Smith, L. L. (1996). Interactive computer software: The effects on young children's reading achievement. *Reading Psychology, 17*(1), 43–64.

Harris, A., & Sipay, E. (1990). *How to increase reading ability: A guide to developmental and remedial methods.* New York: Longman.

Harris, T., & Hodges, R. (Eds.). (1995). *The literacy dictionary: The vocabulary of reading and writing.* Newark, DE: International Reading Association.

Introini-Collision, I., Miyazaki, B., & McGaugh, J. (1991). Involvement of the amygdala in memory-enhancing. *Psychopharmacology, 104*(4), 541–544.

Jacobs, B., Schall, M., & Scheibel, A. B. (1993). A quantitative dendritic analysis of Wernicke's area in humans: Gender, hemispheric and environmental factors. *Journal of Comparative Neurology, 327*(1), 91–111.

Juel, C. (2006). Keys to early reading success: Word recognition and meaning vocabulary. My Sidewalks on Scott Foresman Reading Street presentation. Upper Saddle River, NJ: Pearson Scott Foresman.

Kandel, E. (2006). *In search of memory*. New York: Norton.

Kinomura, L., Larsson, J., Gulyas, A., & Roland, L. (1996). Activation by attention of the human reticular formation and thalamic intralaminar nuclei. *Science, 271*(5248), 512–514.

Kinzer, C., & Leu, D. J., Jr. (1997). The challenge of change: Exploring literacy and learning in electronic environments. *Language Arts, 74* (2), 126–136.

Krashen, S. (1989). We acquire vocabulary and spelling by reading: Additional evidence for the input hypothesis. *The Modern Language Journal, 73*(4), 440–464.

Kutner, M., Greenberg, E., Jin, Y., Boyle, B., Hsu,Y., and Dunleavy, E. (2007). *Literacy in Everyday Life: Results From the 2003 National Assessment of Adult Literacy* (NCES 2007–480). U. S. Department of Education. Washington, DC: National Center for Education Statistics.

Learning First Alliance. (1998). *Every child reading: An action plan*. Alexandria, VA: ASCD.

Long, D., & Chong, J. (2001). Comprehension skill and global coherence: A paradoxical picture of poor comprehenders' abilities. *Journal of Experimental Psychology: Learning, Memory, and Cognition, 27*, 1424–1429.

Mazziotta, J., et al., (2001). A four-dimensional probabilistic atlas of the human brain. *Journal of the American Medical Informatics Association, 8,* 401–430.

McCandliss, B., Cohen, L., & Dehaene, S. (2003). The visual word form area: Expertise for reading in the fusiform gyrus. *Trends in Cognitive Sciences, 7*(7), 293–299.

McGaugh, J., McIntyre, C., & Power, A. (2002). Amygdala modulation of memory consolidation: Interaction with other brain systems. *Neurobiology of Learning and Memory, 78*(3), 539–552.

McKeown, M. G., & I. L. Beck (1988). Learning vocabulary: Different ways for different goals. *Remedial and Special Education, 9*(1), 42–46.

Meyer, L. (2000). Barriers to meaningful instruction for English learners. *Theory into Practice, 39*(4), 228–36.

Meyer, M. S., & Felton, R. H. (1999). Repeated reading to enhance fluency: Old approaches and new directions. *Annals of Dyslexia, 49*(1), 283–306.

Misra, M., Katzir, T., Wolf, M., & Poldrack, R. A. (2004). Neural systems for rapid automatized naming in skilled readers: Unraveling the RAN-reading relationship. *Scientific Studies of Reading, 8*(3), 241–256.

Montague, P., Hyman, S., & Cohen, J. (2004). Computational roles for dopamine in behavioral control. *Nature, 431*(14), 760–769.

Nagy, W. (1988). Teaching vocabulary to improve reading comprehension. Urbana, IL: National Council of Teachers of English.

Nation, K., & Snowling, M. (2004). Beyond phonological skills: broader language skills contribute to the development of reading. *Journal of Research in Reading, 27*(4), 342–356.

National Reading Panel. (2000). *Teaching children to read: An evidence-based assessment of the scientific research literature on reading and its implications for reading instruction: Reports of the subgroups.* Bethesda, MD: National Institute of Child Health and Human Development.

Nature Neuroscience. (2004). Better reading through brain research (Editorial). *Nature Neuroscience, 7,*1.

Nummela, R., & Rosengren, T. (1986). What's happening in students' brains may redefine teaching. *Educational Leadership, 43*(8), 49–53.

Ochs, L. G., et al. (2005). Differential response to reading intervention based on initial skill level, *Annual Meeting of the Cognitive Neuroscience Society,* New York.

Ogle, D. (1986). K–W–L: A teaching model that develops active reading of expository text. *The Reading Teacher, 39*(6), 564–571.

Ornstein, R., & Sobel, D. (1987). *The healing brain: Breakthrough discoveries about how the brain keeps us healthy.* New York: Simon and Schuster.

Patrick, B. C., Skinner, E. A., & Connell, J. P. (1993). What motivates children's behavior and emotion? Joint effects of perceived control and autonomy in the academic domain. *Journal of Personality and Social Psychology, 65,* 781–791.

Pawlak, R., Magarinos, A., Melchor, J., McEwen, B., & Strickland, S. (2003). The amygdala and stress-induced anxiety-like behavior. *Nature Neuroscience, 2,* 168–174.

Peregoy, S., & Boyle, O. (2005). Reading, writing and learning in ESL: A resource book for K–12 teachers. Boston: Pearson Education.

Perfetti, C. A., & Bolger, D. J. (2004). The brain might read that way. *Scientific Studies of Reading, 8*(3), 293–304.

Peterson, P. L., Carpenter, T. P., & Fennema, E. (1988). Teachers' knowledge of students' knowledge in mathematics problem solving: Correlation and case analysis. *Journal of Educational Psychology, 91*(4) 558-569.

Phelps, E. A., Hyder, F., Blamire, A. M., & Shulman, R. G. (1997). FMRI of the prefrontal cortex during overt verbal fluency. *NeuroReport, 8*(2), 561–565.

Poldrack, R., Clark, J. Pare-Blagoev, E. Shohamy, D., Myano, J., Myers, C., et al. (2001). Interactive memory systems in the human brain. *Nature, 414,* 546–550.

Poldrack, R., & Wagner, A. (2004). What can neuroimaging tell us about the mind? Insights from prefrontal cortex. *Current Directions in Psychological Science, 13*(5), 177–181.

Pollatsek, A., & Rayner, K. (1990). Eye movements and lexical access in reading. In D. A. Balota, G. B. Flores d'Arcais, & K. Rayner (Eds.) *Comprehension processes in reading.* Hillsdale, NJ: Lawrence Erlbaum.

Price, S., Moore, C., & Frackowiak, R. (1996). The effect of varying stimulus rate and duration on brain activity during reading. *Neuroimage, 3*(1), 40–52.

Rizzolatti, R., Fogassi, L., & Gallese, V. (2001). Neurophysiological mechanisms underlying the understanding and imitation of action. *Nature Reviews Neuroscience, 2*(9), 661–670.

Roit, M. (2002). *Open court professional development guide: Vocabulary.* Columbus, OH: SRA/McGraw-Hill.

Routman, R. (2000). Conversations: Strategies for teaching, learning, and evaluating. Portsmouth, NH: Heinemann.

Rutter, M. (1985). Resilience in the face of adversity: Protective factors and resilience to psychiatric disorder. *British Journal of Psychiatry, 147,* 608.

Sandak, R., & Poldrack, R. A. (2004). The cognitive neuroscience of reading. *Scientific Studies of Reading, 8*(3).

Santa, C., & Hoien, T. (1999). An assessment of early steps: A program for early intervention of reading problems. *Reading Research Quarterly, 34*(1), 54–79.

Schmeck, R. (1988). Individual differences and learning strategies. In C. E. Weinstein, E. T. Goete, & P. A. Alexander (Eds.), *Learning and study strategies: Issues in assessment, instruction, and evaluation* (pp. 171–191). San Diego, CA: Academic Press.

Schneider, W., & Chein, J. M. (2003). Controlled and automatic processing: Behavior, theory, and biological mechanisms. *Cognitive Science, 27*(3), 525–559.

Sharp, D. L. M., Bransford, J. D., Goldman, S. R., Risko, V. J., Kinzer, C. K., & Vye, N. J. (1995). Dynamic visual support for story comprehension and mental model building by young, at-risk children. *Educational Technology Research and Development, 43,* 25–42.

Siok, W., Perfetti, C., Jin, Z., & Tan, L. (2004). Biological abnormality of impaired reading is constrained by culture. *Nature, 431,* 71–76.

Snow, C. E., Burns, S. M., & Griffin, P. (Eds.). (1998). *Preventing reading difficulties in young children.* Washington, DC: National Academy Press.

Stahl, S. (1999). *Vocabulary development.* Cambridge, MA: Brookline Books.

Stahl, S., & Fairbanks, M. (Spring, 1986). The effects of vocabulary instruction: A model-based meta-analysis. *Review of Educational Research, 56*(1), 72–110.

Stanovich, K. E., & Siegel, L. S. (1994). Phenotypic performance profile of children with reading disabilities: A regression-based test of the phonological-core variable-difference model. *Journal of Educational Psychology, 86,* 24–53.

Swain, M., & Lapkin, S. (1995). Problems in output and the cognitive processes they generate: A step towards second language learning. *Applied Linguistics, 16,* 371-391.

Tallal, P., Merzenich, M., Jenkins, W. M., & Miller, S. L. (1999). Moving research from the laboratory to clinics and classrooms. In D. D. Duane (Ed.), *Reading and attention disorders* (pp. 93–112). Baltimore: York Press.

Temple, E., Deutsch, G. K., Poldrack, R. A., Miller, S. L., Tallal, P., Merzenich, M. M., & Gabriel, J. (2003). Neural deficits in children with dyslexia ameliorated by behavioral remediation: Evidence from *f*MRI. *Proceedings of the National Academy of Sciences, 100*(5), 2860–2865.

Thierry, G., Boulanouar, K., Kherif, F., Ranjeva, J., & Demonte, J. (1999). Temporal sorting of neural components underlying phonological processing. *NeuroReport, 10*(12), 2599–2603.

Thierry, G., Giraud, A., & Price, C. (2003). Hemispheric dissociation in access to the human semantic system. *Neuron, 38*(3), 499–506.

Turkeltaub, P. E., Gareau, L., Flowers, D. L., Zeffiro, T. A., & Eden, G. F. (2003). Development of neural mechanisms for reading. *Nature Neuroscience, 6*(7), 767–773.

Vellutino, F., Fletcher, J., Snowling, M., & Scanlon, D. (2004). Specific reading disability (dyslexia): What have we learned in the past four decades? *Journal of Child Psychology and Psychiatry, 45*, 2–40.

Vygotsky, L. S. (1978). Interaction between learning and development. In M. Cole, V. John-Steiner, S. Scribner, & E. Souberman (Eds.). *Mind in society: The development of higher psychological processes* (pp. 191–197). Cambridge, MA: Harvard University Press.

Wagner, A., Schacter, D., Rotte, M., Koutstaal, W., Maril, A., Dale, A. M., Rosen, B., & Buckner, R. (1998). Building memories: Remembering and forgetting of verbal experiences as predicted by brain activity. *Science, 281*, 1185–1190

Wagner, R., Torgesen, J., & Rashotte, C. (1994). Development of reading-related phonological processing abilities: New evidence of bi-directional causality from a latent variable longitudinal study. *Developmental Psychology, 30,* 73–87.

Wagner, R. K., Torgesen, J. K., Rashotte, C. A., Hecht, S. A., Barker, T. A., Burgess, S., Donahue, R. J., & Garon, T. (1997). Changing relations between phonological processing abilities and word-level reading as children develop from beginning to skilled readers: A 5-year longitudinal study. *Developmental Psychology, 33*(3), 468–479.

Wesson, K. (2006). Drawing and the brain: Visualizing information is a vital early step in learning to read. *American School Board Journal, 193*(6), 40–42.

Wigfield, A. (1994). The role of children's achievement values in the self-regulation of their learning outcomes. In D. H. Schunk & B. J. Zimmerman (Eds.), *Self-regulation of learning and performance: Issues and educational applications* (pp. 101–124). Mahwah, NJ: Erlbaum.

Willis, J. (2005). Highlighting for understanding of complex college text. *The National Teaching and Learning Forum.*

Wolf, M., Goldberg, A., O'Rourke, A., Gidney, C., Lovett, M., Cirino, P., & Morris, R. (2002). The second deficit: An investigation of the independence of phonological and naming-speed deficits in developmental dyslexia. *Reading and Writing, 15,* 43–72.

Yaniv, D., Vouimba, R., Diamond, D., & Richter–Levin, G. (2003). Amygdala in brain function. *Journal of Neuroscience, 23*(11), 4406–4409.

Index

activating prior knowledge, 129–130
affective filter (amygdala), 82, 85–91
alphabetic principle, 20, 23
amygdala, 69, 79, 82
angular gyri, 19
angular temporal gyri, 15
assessment
    progress *vs.* product, 68–69
    using, 24
attention deficit hyperactivity disorder, 94
axons, 93–94

background knowledge, 132
Ballard, Melissa, 154–155
big picture, 130, 132
Blau, Sheridan, 153
bodily-kinesthetic intelligence, 64
book reports, 74
brain-based learning research
    evaluation of, 6–9
    future prospects, 157–158
    Guided Reading (software), 66–67
    imaging techniques, 2–3
    intervention selection, 66–67
    metaphor construction activity, 106
    multiple reading networks, 48–49
    peer review, 5
    reading comprehension, 149
    The Reading Works (software), 66–67
    regional brain subspecialization, 49–50

brain-based learning research *(continued)*
    sources of, and information from, 4–6
    standards and practice, 44–46
    visual and verbal memory, 117
    vocabulary building, 91–93, 100, 106, 122–123
brain development, infant, 13
brain glitch theory, 7
brain plasticity, 35–36
brain wave speed measurement (qEEG), 18, 49
Broca's area, 12, 15, 117, 149

categorization
    brain activity and, 49
    and meaning, 31–33
    as patterns, 27–30
    and vocabulary building, 103–105
celebrations, unit, 76
Challenge and Exploration, as theme, 72–76
Chinese language reading, 15
choice, in materials, 75–76
choral reading, 59
classroom environment, 68–69
cloze sentences, 114
compare and contrast, 137–138
compound word formation, 26–27
comprehension. *See* reading comprehension

computers
  building patterning skills with,
    42–44
  and fluency practice, 77–78
  recording software, 62
  software, 62, 66–67, 77–78
concept definition maps, 113–114
cultural load, 102–103

decoding words, 127, 128
dendrites, 36, 93–94
differentiation, 4, 54–55
discussion, student-centered, 69–71
dopamine, 60, 79, 93–98
dorsal posterior reading system, 15, 19

electronic whiteboards, 77
electrophysiological methods, 17
emotions, and performance, 69, 85–91
English Language Learners, 89, 90,
  101–102
Ethics, as theme, 71–72, 112–113
event-related potentials (ERPs), 17
explicit memory, 148

flashcards, 54, 99, 113
foreign language instruction, 124
frontal lobe, 94
frontal reading system, 14
functional magnetic resonance imaging
  (fMRI)
  and memory studies, 148
  and parallel reading networks, 48–51
  uses of, 2–3

GarageBand, 62
Gardner, Howard, 62
gaze-following, 13
glucose metabolism, brain, 3, 5–6
graphic organizers, 30
  KWL, 39–42, 130, 133–134
  reading comprehension, 141–142
  vocabulary building, 113–114
  web sites for, 142
grouping, 54
Guided Reading (software), 66–67
guided rereading, 56–57

hemoglobin, 3
high-frequency words, 98–99
highlighting text, 152–155
hippocampus, 22, 56, 117
homework, 121
human development, 2

illustrations, 109–110
imitation learning, 12–14
implicit memory, 148
independent reading, 121–123
infant brain development, 13
inferences, 138
Input Hypothesis, 91–92, 122–123
instructional strategies
  building memory for comprehension,
    148–152
  categorization, 27–30, 103–105
  category and meaning activity, 31–33
  dopamine release, 95–98
  evaluating success of, 44–46
  fluency-building, 59–67
  highlighting text for comprehension,
    152–155
  informed by research, 4–6
  note taking, 146–147
  patterning, 23–24, 105–108
  phonemic awareness, 19–21, 25–27
  prediction and patterning, 37–42
  reading comprehension, 135–139
  repetition, 25
  vocabulary and patterning, 105–108
  vocabulary review, 118–122
  vocabulary word preview, 101–102
intelligence, and reading, 17–18
interest inventories, 73, 83, 84
International Consortium for Brain
  Mapping (ICBM), 157
interpersonal intelligence, 65
intrapersonal intelligence, 65

journals. See literature logs

KWL activities, 39–42, 130, 133–134

language bath, 90
language development, 2, 12–14

learning styles
    discovering, 131
    redundant instruction to accommodate, 28–29
    and vocabulary building, 115–116
linguistic intelligence, 63
listening competence, 115
literature, rich and meaningful, 122–123
literature logs, 144–145
logical-mathematical intelligence, 63–64
lower frontal lobe, 16

magnetoencephalography (MEG), 17
Mazziotta, John, 157
memory
    and brain plasticity, 36
    building activities, 150–152
    mnemonics, 151–152
    neural connections and long-term, 116–117
    and reading comprehension, 147–149
    repetition and pattern manipulation, 27
    verbal, 117
    visual, 117
    working memory networks, 48–49, 116, 147–148
mental models. See visualization
metacognition, 37, 155–156
middle school, vocabulary building, 123–124
mirror neuron activation, 12–14
mnemonics, 151–152
modeling
    comprehension strategies, 139–140
    fluent reading, 57–58
    note taking, 145–146
    supportive reading, 58
motivation, student, 82–83, 84–85, 129
multiple intelligences
    and reading fluency, 62–65
    and vocabulary building, 114–115, 118–119
music, 91
musical-rhythmic intelligence, 63

naming practice, repeated, 52–53, 100

naturalist intelligence, 62
neocortex, 11
neuroimaging
    applicability to reading research, 4–6
    extent of information through, 7–8
    techniques, 2–3
neuron networks, 30–31
neurotransmitters, 93–98. See also dopamine
No Child Left Behind, 4
note taking, 145–147, 152–155

occipital lobes, 47
oral communication, 2
oral reading
    in book reports, 74
    choral reading, 59
    and fluency, 47–48
    guided rereading, 56–57
    modeling fluent reading, 57–58
    modeling supportive reading, 58
    partner reading, 60–61
    repeated reading, 54–55
    stress reduction, 68–69, 79
    student-adult reading, 59
    tape-assisted reading, 61–62
Output Hypothesis, 92–93

parents, advising, 8
parietal lobe, 15
participation, student, 87–89
partner reading, 60–61, 74
patterning
    and brain plasticity, 35–36
    categorization, 27–30, 103–105
    computer-assisted, 42–44
    prediction and previewing, 36–42
    reading research on, 23
    recognition strategies, 23–27
    using learned patterns, 29–30
    and vocabulary, 33–34
    of vocabulary, 105–108
peer teaching, 143–144
people with differences, respecting, 57–58
personally meaningful experiences
    and reading comprehension, 138, 145

personally meaningful experiences
(continued)
  vocabulary building, 101–102,
    112–113
phonemic awareness
  activities that build, 19–21
  neural mechanisms of, 16–18
  phoneme-to-grapheme correspon-
    dence, 23–24, 25
phonics instruction, 7, 126
phonological processing, 18–19, 100
plasticity, brain, 35–36
positron emission tomography (PET)
  first research results from, 5–6
  and parallel reading networks, 48–51
  uses of, 2–3
prediction
  and patterning, 36–42
  in reading, 133–134
prefrontal cortex, 50, 117
prefrontal lobe, 11, 22
prereading, 131–133
previewing
  activating prior knowledge, 129–130
  previewing text, and patterning,
    36–42
  vocabulary word preview, 99–102
prior knowledge, activating, 129–130
puzzlemaker.com, 121

R.A.D., 79
rapid automatized naming (RAN), 17,
  51–53
reading
  extensive exposure to, 122–123
  goals, 132–133
  independent, 121–123
  individual variation in process, 12
  interrelated phases of, 11
  and phonological processing, 18–19
reading comprehension
  about, 126–127
  decoding, 127, 128
  graphic organizers for, 141–142
  highlighting text, 152–155
  independent activities, 144–145
  literature logs, 144–145
  memory and, 147–152

metacognition, 155–156
  motivators, 129–130
  note taking, 145–147
  peer teaching, 143–144
  predicting, 133–134
  prereading, 131–133
  reciprocal reading, 143
  strategies, 135–139
  strategy goals, 127–128
  teacher modeling, 139–140
reading difficulties
  brain glitch theory of, 7
  and general intelligence, 17–18
  incidence, 2
reading out loud. *See* oral reading
The Reading Works (software), 66–67
reciprocal reading, 143
repeated reading, 54–55
repetition, 25–26
research, brain-based learning. *See* brain-
  based learning research
responses, to peer reading, 58, 61
Rizzollati, Giaccamo, 12
rote memorization, 98–99

scientific vocabulary, 34
screening, 24
self-monitoring, 138–139
sensory input
  and vocabulary building, 114
sequential learning, 90
skits, 75–76
software. *See* computer software
sound and hearing, 16. *See also* phonemic
  awareness
spatial reasoning skills, 24
speech, processing. *See* phonological processing
speech synthesizers, 78
SSPC procedure, 61
story prediction activity, 38–42
story webs, 142
strategies, brain-based reading
  caution implementing, 8
stress
  and fluency, 68–69, 79
  and receptiveness, 87
  and sensory input, 83, 85–86

student-adult reading, 59
students
    motivation, 82–83, 84–85, 129
    participation, 87–89
    self-confidence, 68–69
    student-adult reading, 59
    student-centered discussion, 69–71
student self-confidence, 68–69
studies, research, 44–46
summarization, 136–137
supramarginal temporal gyri, 15
synonyms, 114

tape-assisted reading, 61–62
teachers. *See also* instructional strategies
    informed and qualified, 4
    modeling comprehension strategies,
        139–140
technology
    computer adjuncts to fluency prac-
        tice, 77–78
    computer recording software, 62
    computers and patterning skills,
        42–44
    computer software, 62, 66–67,
        77–78
    electronic whiteboards, 77
    for reading fluency, 65–66
temporal lobe, 15, 47, 149
text selections, 85, 104, 126
thematic units, cross-curricular, 71–76
thesaurus use, 123
timelines, 141
total physical response (TPR), 87, 115

UCLA (University of California, Los
    Angeles), 5–6

Venn diagrams, 141
ventral posterior processing system,
    14–15
verbal fluency, 50
visual art activities, 24
visualization, for vocabulary building,
    109–112
visual organizers, 30, 105
    KWL, 39–42, 130, 133–134
    reading comprehension, 141–142

visual organizers *(continued)*
    vocabulary building, 113–114
    web sites for, 142
visual-spatial intelligence, 64
visual word form area (VWFA), 15
visual word pattern recognition, 14–15
vocabulary
    and patterning, 33–34
    pre-instruction in reading, 131–132
    student-centered discussion, 69–71
    vocabulary gap, 80–81
vocabulary building
    about, 80, 124–125
    and affective filtering, 85–91
    brain processes in, 81–82
    categorization and, 103–105
    components, 82–83
    and dopamine release, 93–98
    graphic organizers, 113–114
    high frequency words, 98–99
    implicit learning through reading,
        122–123
    middle school, 123–124
    and patterning, 105–108
    personalization, 112–113
    physical movement and, 114
    reinforcement, 118
    resonance through motivation,
        82–83, 84–85
    review, 118–122
    roots, prefixes, and suffixes, 108–109,
        124
    sensory experiences and, 114
    theories for, 91–93
    visualization, 109–112
    vocabulary-rich speaking, 115–116
    word preview, 99–102

word maps, 113
word patterns, 25–26
word recognition speed, 51–54
working memory networks, 48–49, 116,
    147–148. *See also* memory

zones of actual development (ZAD), 143
zones of proximal development (ZPD),
    31, 142

About the Author

Dr. Judy Willis, a board-certified neurologist and middle school teacher in Santa Barbara, California, has combined her training in neuroscience and neuroimaging with her teacher education training and years of classroom experience. She has become an authority in the field of learning-centered brain research and classroom strategies derived from this research.

After graduating Phi Beta Kappa as the first woman graduate of Williams College (in 1971), Willis attended UCLA School of Medicine, where she remained as a resident and ultimately became Chief Resident in Neurology. She practiced neurology for 15 years, and then received a credential and master's degree in education from the University of California, Santa Barbara. She has taught in elementary, middle, and graduate schools; was a fellow in the National Writing Project; and currently teaches at Santa Barbara Middle School.

Her first book, *Research Based Strategies to Ignite Student Learning*, was published by ASCD in 2006, and her second book, *Brain-Friendly Strategies for the Inclusion Classroom*, followed in 2007. Willis gives presentations throughout the world about brain research-based learning strategies, and her articles have been published in a multitude of magazines, journals, and newspapers across the United States and internationally. She is a member of the Hawn Foundation board of directors, and she travels around the world with actress Goldie Hawn to make presentations about mindful teaching and learning.

Willis writes a weekly wine column, and along with her husband, Dr. Paul Willis, also a neurologist, makes prize-winning wine at home under the label *Chateau Huit Feet,* named in tribute to the eight feet of the Willis family that stomp the grapes. You can contact her at jwillisneuro@aol.com or visit her Web site at RADTeach.com.

Related ASCD Resources: Literacy

At the time of publication, the following resources were available; for the most up-to-date information about ASCD resources, go to www.ascd.org. ASCD stock numbers are noted in parentheses.

Mixed Media

The Multiple Intelligences of Reading and Writing: Making the Words Come Alive Books-in-Action Package (10 Books and 1 Video) by Thomas Armstrong (#703381)

Using Data to Assess Your Reading Program (Book and CD-ROM) by Emily Calhoun (#102268)

Networks

Visit the ASCD Web site (www.ascd.org) and click on About ASCD. Go to the section on Networks for information about professional educators who have formed groups around topics such as "Language, Literacy, and Literature" and "Brain-Compatible Learning." Look in the Network Directory for current facilitators' addresses and phone numbers.

Online Courses

Visit the ASCD Web site (www.ascd.org) for the following professional development opportunities:

Helping Struggling Readers by Kathy Checkley

Six Research-Based Literacy Approaches for the Elementary Classroom by Kristen Nelson

Successful Strategies for Literacy and Learning by Angelika Machi

Print Products

Building Student Literacy Through Sustained Silent Reading by Steve Gardiner (#105027)

Educational Leadership, March 2004: What Research Says About Reading (Entire Issue #104028)

Educational Leadership, October 2005: Reading Comprehension (Entire Issue #106037)

Research-Based Methods of Reading Instruction, Grades K–3 by Sharon Vaugh and Sylvia Linan-Thompson (#104134)

Video

Implementing a Reading Program in Secondary Schools (One 30-Minute Videotape with a Facilitator's Guide #402033)

The Lesson Collection: Literacy Strategies Tapes 49-56 (Eight 10- to 20-Minute Videotapes #405160)

For more information, visit us on the World Wide Web (http://www.ascd.org), send an e-mail message to member@ascd.org, call the ASCD Service Center (1-800-933-ASCD or 703-578-9600, then press 2), send a fax to 703-575-5400, or write to Information Services, ASCD, 1703 N. Beauregard St., Alexandria, VA 22311-1714 USA.